Bariatric Air Fryer

Cookbook for Beginners on a Budget

2023 Edition

2000-Day of Tasty Recipes that Anyone Can do in 30 mins to Maintain Your New Stomach Healthy and Stay in Shape
60-day Gastric Sleeve Meal Plan

By

Wilda Buckley

TABLE OF CONTENTS

INTRODUCTION 9

CHAPTER 1: LEARN EVERYTHING THERE IS TO KNOW ABOUT THE BARIATRIC DIET AND THE AIR FRYER 10

1.1 What is the Bariatric diet? 10

1.2 Health Advantages of a Bariatric Diet 10

1.3 Foods to Consume and Foods to Avoid: 11

1.4 Suggestions for Getting Started 14

1.5 Making the Most of Your Post-Surgery Life ... 16

1.6 Foods to Avoid and Final Recommendations 17

1.7 What is the Air fryer? 20

1.8 Advantages of Air Frying 20

1.9 Cleaning your Air Fryer 21

CHAPTER 2: BREAKFAST RECIPES 24

1. Scrambled Breakfast Eggs 24

2. Tasty Breakfast Eggplant Pizza 24

3. Classic Air Fried Breakfast Frittata 24

4. Avocado Cauliflower Toast 25

5. Air Fried Cheesy Egg Bites 25

6. Air Fryer Breakfast Apple Protein Muffins ... 25

7. Chanterelle Mushrooms and Zucchini Omelet 26

8. Breakfast Portobello Pizzas 26

9. Cheesy Cauliflower Hash Browns 26

10. Breakfast Feta and Spinach Casserole 27

11. Healthy and Crunchy Breakfast Granola 27

12. Creamy Veggie Breakfast Frittata 27

13. Cheese, Egg and Bacon Roll-Ups 28

14. Crustless Breakfast Quiche 28

15. Breakfast Mashed Potato Pancakes 28

16. Cheese and Ham Omelet 29

17. Low-Carb Air Fried Garlic Bread 29

18. Sugar-Free Air fried Mix Berries Oatmeal 29

19. Italian-Style Air Fried Breakfast Eggs 30

20. Mushrooms and Taleggio Omelet 30

21. Cheesy Chicken, Carrot and Spinach Omelet 30

22. Crustless Breakfast Caprese Quiche 31

23. Air Fried Caprese Stuffed Avocado 31

24. Fluffy Air Fried Courgette Omelet 32

25. Classic Air fried Egg Casserole 32

26. Air Fryer Cheese Picante Omelet Pie 32

27. Air Fryer Avocado Egg Boat 33

28. Air Fried Sheet Pan Eggs 33

29. Air Fried Buffalo Breakfast Egg Cups 33

30. Air Fried Breakfast Farmer's Casserole 33

CHAPTER 3: APPETIZER AND SNACK RECIPES 35

1. Air Fried Parmesan Garlic Oil-Free Chips 35

2. Air Fried Cheddar-Sausage Bites 35

3. Air Fried Stuffed Cherry Peppers 36

4. Air Fried Stuffed Mini Sweet Peppers 36

5. Bacon Wrapped Brussels Sprouts 36

6. Air Fried Crispy Salmon Jerky 37

7. Air Fried Seasoned Apple Chips 37

8. Air Fried Baba Ghanoush (Lebanese Appetizer) 37

9. Air Fried Cheesy Popcorn 38

10. Air Fried Cheesy Cauliflower Bread Sticks 38

11. Crispy Bacon Wrapped Asparagus 39

12. Air Fried Parmesan Cheddar Crisps 39

13. Air Fried Kale Chips 39

14. Air Fried Asparagus Tots 40

15. Air Fried Cheesy Crackers 40

16. Air Fried Deviled Eggs 40

17. Air Fried Falafel 41

18. Air Fried Pizza Muffins 41

19. Air Fried Garlic-Almond Crackers 42

20. Air Fried Bacon Wrapped Scallops 42

21. Air Fried Sausage Stuffed Mushrooms 43

22. Air-Fried Zucchini Bites 43

23. Cheesy Pizza Pepperoni Puffs 43

24. Air Fried Cheesy Olives 44

25. Air Fried Brie and Artichoke 44

26. Apple Fritters with Cinnamon Sprinkle Topping 44

27. Air Fryer Loaded Faux-Tato Skins 45

28. Air Fried Tasty Pickles 45

29. Air Fried Mozzarella Cheese Balls 46

30. Air Fried Cheesy Bacon Jalapeno Bread 46

CHAPTER 4: LUNCH AND MAIN RECIPES 47

1. Air Fried Zucchini Skins with Buffalo Chicken 47

2. Air Fryer Cauliflower Steak Loaded 47

3. Air Fried Three Cheese Stuffed Zucchini Boats 48

4. Air Fried Roasted Broccoli Salad 48

5. Air Fried Cheesy Chicken Mushroom 48

6. Air Fried Peppers and Chicken 49

7. Air Fried Greek-Style Chicken Stir Fry 49

8. Air Fried Turkey Burgers 50

9. Air Fried Roasted Whole Lemon Cauliflower 50

10. Air Fried Cheese Garlic Rolls 50

11. Air Fried Stir-Fry Broccoli and Beef 51

12. Air Fried Spinach Gratin 51

13. Classic Air Fried Green Bean Casserole 52

14. Air Fried Ranch Chicken Bacon Casserole 52

15. Air Fried Zucchini and Halloumi Frittata 52

16. Air Fried Green Chili Casserole 53

17. Air Fried Classic Meatloaf 53

18. Air Fryer Feta and Spinach Pie 53

19. Air Fried Cloud Bread 54

20. Air Fried Creamy Broccoli and Chicken Casserole .. 54

21. Air Fried Healthy Chicken and Veggies 54

22. Air Fried Stuffed Flounder 55

23. Air Fried Crispy Pork Chop Salad 55

24. Air Fried Cajun Chicken Tenders 56

25. Air Fried Delicious Shrimp Kebabs 56

26. Air Fried Chicken Fajitas 56

27. Air Fried Chicken Lunch Patties 57

28. Air Fried Fajita-Flavored Flank Steak Rolls 57

29. Air Fried Leek Egg and Ham Cups 57

30. Air Fried Italian Mushroom and Asparagus Frittata 58

CHAPTER 5: FISH AND SEAFOOD RECIPES 59

1. Air Fried Healthy Salmon with Fennel Salad 59

2. Air Fried Tuna Steak with Sesame Crust 59

3. Air Fried Red Pepper Sauce Scallops 60

4. Air Fried Fish Lentil Patties 60

5. Air Fried Scallops with Herbs and Cheese 60

6. Air Fried Mussels with Herb and Lemon 61

7. Air Fried Tikka-Style Fish 61

8. Air Fried Southwestern Catfish 61

9. Air Fried COD with Asparagus 62

10. Air Fried Parchment Wrapped Orange Tilapia ... 62

11. Air Fried Shrimp and Tomatoes with Sauce 62

12. Air Fried Crispy Salmon Patties 63

13. Air Fried Tasty Firecracker Shrimp 63

14. Air Fried Creamy Tuna Casserole 63

15. Air Fried Foil Packed Lobster Tails 64

16. Air Fried Scallion Sea Bass 64

17. Air Fried Herb-Crusted Salmon 65

18. Air Fried Seafood Gratin 65

19. Air Fried Pecan-Crusted Tilapia 65

20. Air Fried Steelhead Trout with Garlic, Lemon and Rosemary 66

21. Air Fried Lobster and Crab Stuffed Mushrooms 66

22. Air Fried Shrimp Scampi 66

23. Air Fryer Southwestern Style Scallops 67

24. Air Fried Blue Cheese-Stuffed Shrimp 67

25. Air Fried Seafood Filled Zucchini 67

26. Air Fried Greek-Style Fish Fillets 68

27. Air Fried Flounder with Stuffing 68

28. Air Fryer Cheese Herbed Salmon Frittata 69

29. Air Fried Salmon, Zucchini, and Carrot Patties 69

30. Air Fried Prawns with Garlic, Tomato, and Herb 69

CHAPTER 6: VEGETABLE RECIPES 71

1. Air Fried Spicy Stir-Fry Cauliflower 71

2. Potato and Kale Air Fryer Nuggets 71

3. Air Fried Asian Green Bean 72

4. Air Fried Chipotle Flavored Asparagus 72

5. Air Fried Tasty Butternut Squash 72

6. Air Fryer Roasted Cauliflower with Cilantro and Lime 73

7. Air Fried Cauliflower Cheese Tots 73

8. Air Fried Root Vegetables 73

9. Air Fryer Tasty Zucchini Casserole 74

10. Healthy and Tasty Air Fried Broccoli Tots 74

11. Air Fried Celery Sticks 75

12. Air Fried Ratatouille 75

13. Air Fried Vegetable Tofu 75

14. Air Fried Okra 76

15. Air Fried Broccoli Casserole 76

16. Air Fried Greek-Style Stuffed Eggplant 76

17. Air Fryer Roasted Veggie Bowl 77

18. Air Fryer Roasted Loaded Broccoli 77

19. Air Fried Asparagus with Cheese Sauce 77

20. Air Fried Cheesy Herbed Cauliflower Quinoa Casserole 78

21. Air Fried Eggplant Tomato Casserole 78

22. Air Fried Sweet Corn Custard 78

23. Air Fried Vegetables and Cheese Skewers 79

24. Air Fried Vegetable Frittata 79

25. Air Fried Tasty and Crispy Artichoke Fries 80

26. Air Fried BBQ Flavored Soy Curls 80

27. Air Fried Parmesan-Herb Tomatoes 80

28. Air Fryer Roasted Basil Red Peppers 81

29. Air Fryer Seasoned Eggplant 81

30. Air Fried Eggplant with Cherry Tomatoes and Herbs 81

CHAPTER 7: BEEF RECIPES 83

1. Air Fried Sirloin Steak with Thyme and Garlic 83

2. Air Fried Grilled Spiced Steak and Vegetables 83

3. Air Fried Carne Asada 83

4. Air Fried Russian Beef 84

5. Air Fried Peppercorn-Crusted Beef Tenderloin 84

6. Air Fryer Roasted Beef with Onion Gravy 84

7. Air Fried Spicy Beef Strips with Peas 85

8. Air Fried Chipotle Steaks 85

9. Air Fried Steak with Chimichurri 85

10. Air Fried Korean Style Rib Barbecue 86

11. Air Fried Maple Mustard Beef Steaks 86

12. Air Fryer Grilled Flank Steaks with Chili 87

13. Air Fried Seared Beef Ribeye 87

14. Air Fried Beef Yakitori 87

15. Air Fried Beef Bulgur Patties 88

16. Air Fried Garlic Butter Flavored Steak Bites 88

17. Air Fried Mini Meatloaf Muffins 88

18. Air Fried Soy Ginger Beef Skewers 89

19. Air Fried Beef Tagliata 89

20. Air Fried Beef Patties Smothered in Mushrooms Sauce 89

21. Air Fried Beef Tenderloin with Garlic Mushroom Sauce 90

22. Air Fried Beef and Egg Bake 90

23. Air Fried Steak Pinwheels 90

24. Air Fried Italian-Style Meatloaf 91

25. Air Fried Thai-Style Beef Tri-Tip 91

26. Air Fryer Corned Beef Brisket 92

27. Air Fried Asian-Style Beef Skewers 92

28. Air Fried Barbarian Beef 92

29. Air Fried Sesame Beef 93

30. Air Fried Greek-Style Meatballs 93

CHAPTER 8: POULTRY RECIPES 94

1. Air-Fried Butter Parmesan Chicken 94

2. Air-Fried Onion Chicken 94

3. Air Fried Delicious Chicken Gratin 94

4. Air Fried Herbed Turkey Meatballs 95

5. Air-Fried Polynesian Kebabs 95

6. Air-Fried Stuffed Turkey Tenderloins 96

7. Air Fried Filipino Adobo Chicken 96

8. Air Fried Chicken Stuffed with Mozzarella and Asparagus 96

9. Air Fried Spicy Buttermilk Chicken 97

10. Air Fried Lemon-Butter Chicken Tenders 97

11. Air Fried Asian-Style Chicken Tandoori 97

12. Air Fried Chicken, Pepper, Bean, Tomato Roast 98

13. Air Fried Peri-Peri Chicken 98

14. Air Fried Whole Roasted Chicken with Vegetables 98

15. Air Fried Chicken Yakitori 99

16. Air Fried Balsamic Chicken 99

17. Air Fried Lemon-Oregano Chicken 100

18. Air Fried Horseradish-Crusted Turkey Tenderloin 100

19. Air Fried Cajun Chicken 100

20. Air Fried Turkey Saltimbocca 101

21. Air Fried Nepiev Chicken 101

22. Air Fried Teriyaki Chicken 101

23. Air Fried Turkey Loaf 102

24. Air Fried Buttery Maple Chicken 102

25. Air Fried Spicy Barbecue Chicken 103

26. Air Fried Chicken Tikka 103

27. Air Fried Drumsticks with Thyme Mustard Sauce 103

28. Air Fried Garlic-Mustard Chicken 104

29. Air Fried Chicken Breast with Veggies 104

30. Air Fried Chicken Meatballs 104

CHAPTER 9: PORK RECIPES 106

1. Air-Fried Pork Chops Stuffed with Mushroom Sauce 106

2. Air-Fried Balsamic Pork Loin 106

3. Air-Fried Pork Tenderloin with Dijon Sauce 106

4. Air-Fried Sheet Pan Pork with Asparagus 107

5. Air Fried Orange Spiced Ham Steak 108

6. Air Fried Pork Tenderloin Stuffed with Pepper 108

7. Air-Fried Sautéed Pork Chops with Garlic Spinach 108

8. Air-Fried Orange-Glazed Pork Loin 109

9. Air-Fried Maple-Glazed Pork Chops 109

10. Air-Fried Pork Stuffed with Cheese, Spinach and Pesto 110

11. Air-Fried Pork Medallions with Balsamic Raspberry Sauce 110

12. Air-Fried Pork Chops with Beans 110

13. Air-Fried Plum-Glazed Pork Kebabs 111

14. Air-Fried Southwestern-Style Pineapple Pork Chops 111

15. Air-Fried Balsamic Glazed Pork and Fig Skewers 111

16. Air-Fried Pork Chop Casserole 112

17. Air-Fried Barbecued Pork Skewers 112

18. Air-Fried Delicious Pork Medallions with Strawberry-Garlic Sauce 113

19. Air-Fried Orange and Curried Pork Kebabs 113

20. Air-Fried One-Pan Pork and Squash 113

CHAPTER 10: DESSERT RECIPES 115

1. Air-Fried Sugar-free Peanut Butter Cookies 115

2. Air-Fried Magic Cookie Bars 115

3. Air-Fried Sugar-Free and Low-Carb Banana Bread 116

4. Air-Fried Chewy Avocado Brownies 116

5. Air-Fried Chocolate Hazelnut Lava Cake 117

6. Air-Fried Low-Carb Banana Muffins 117

7. Air-Fried Lemon Raspberry Loaf 117

8. Air-Fried Gluten-Free Cherry Cobbler with Hazelnut Topping 118

9. Air-Fried Low-Carb Chocolate Chip Zucchini Muffins 118

10. Air-Fried Blueberry Scones 119

11. Air-Fried Gluten-Free Coconut Macaroons............ 119

12. Air-Fried Simple Low-Carb Pound Cake 120

13. Air-Fried Vanilla Cupcakes (Sugar-Free)................... 120

14. Air-Fried Low-Carb Lemon Bars 120

15. Air-Fried Crunchy Butter Cashew Cookies 121

16. Air-Fried Chocolate Almond Flour Cupcakes 121

17. Air-Fried Crunchy Oatmeal Cookies 122

18. Air-Fried Fluffy Cream Cheese Cookies 122

19. Air-Fried Low-Carb Blackberry Cobbler 122

20. Air-Fried Sugar-Free Graham Crackers 123

60 DAYS MEAL PLAN 125

1st Year.. 125

2nd Year 126

3rd Year 127

4th Year 128

CONCLUSION 130

© Copyright 2023 by (Wilda Buckley)- All rights reserved.

This document is geared towards providing exact and reliable information in regards to the topic and issue covered. The publication is sold with the idea that the publisher is not required to render accounting, officially permitted, or otherwise, qualified services. If advice is necessary, legal or professional, a practiced individual in the profession should be ordered.

From a Declaration of Principles, which was accepted and approved equally by a Committee of the American Bar Association and a Committee of Publishers and Associations.

In no way is it legal to reproduce, duplicate, or transmit any part of this document in either electronic means or in printed format. Recording of this publication is strictly prohibited, and any storage of this document is not allowed unless with written permission from the publisher. All rights reserved.

The information provided herein is stated to be truthful and consistent, in that any liability, in terms of inattention or otherwise, by any usage or abuse of any policies, processes, or directions contained within is the solitary and utter responsibility of the recipient reader. Under no circumstances will any legal responsibility or blame be held against the publisher for any reparation, damages, or monetary loss due to the information herein, either directly or indirectly.

Respective authors own all copyrights not held by the publisher.

The information herein is offered for informational purposes solely and is universal as so. The presentation of the information is without contract or any type of guarantee assurance.

The trademarks that are used are without any consent, and the publication of the trademark is without permission or backing by the trademark owner. All trademarks and brands within this book are for clarifying purposes only and are owned by the owners themselves, not affiliated with this document.

INTRODUCTION

You've definitely heard the phrase "bariatric," but what does it actually mean? "Relating to or specialized in the treatment of obesity" is what bariatric refers to. When the term "bariatric" is used in a medical setting, it relates to obesity prevention, treatment, and causes.

The term bariatrics was coined in 1965 from the Greek roots bar- ("weight," as in barometer), -iatr ("treatment," as in pediatrics), and -ic (as in bariatric surgery) ("pertaining to"). This category includes dieting, exercise, and behavioral therapy approaches to weight loss, as well as medicine and surgery.

Bariatrics is a medical specialty that treats obese people with food, exercise, and behavioral treatment to help them lose weight and improve their overall health. When you think about bariatrics, you probably think of bariatric surgery, often known as metabolic or weight-loss surgery.

Obese persons can reduce weight using weight-loss operations such as a Roux-en-Y gastric bypass or a vertical sleeve gastrectomy. Weight-loss surgery can also aid in the prevention or treatment of chronic conditions.

For those looking to improve their health and lose weight, an air fryer is a revolutionary piece of kitchen equipment. Due to their low calorie and fat content, air-fried foods are advertised as a nutritious alternative to traditional deep-fried cuisine. Instead of fully drowning the meal in oil, air-frying needs only a tablespoon to get the same texture and taste as deep-fried foods. They have fewer calories, fat, and potentially hazardous substances than traditional fried dishes. If you're attempting to shed weight or lesser your fat intake, switching to an air fryer rather than the deep fryer might be a great choice.

In this Cookbook, you will discover everything there is to know about the bariatric diet, air fryers, and delicious bariatric air fryer recipes that you can cook and enjoy in your air fryer while on a bariatric diet journey.

Chapter 1:
Learn Everything There Is to Know About the Bariatric Diet and the Air Fryer

1.1 What is the Bariatric diet?

A bariatric diet is a manner of eating that allows your stomach to heal without being stretched by the food you eat after having bariatric surgery. It also helps your body adjust to consuming smaller portions of food that your smaller stomach can absorb easily and safely.

People who have had a sleeve gastrectomy or gastric bypass surgery, also known as a Roux-en-Y gastric bypass, will utilize a bariatric diet for healing and changing their eating habits.

To attain a steady long-term outcome, it is critical to implement a variety of permanent lifestyle adjustments. Your eating habits, attitudes, stress management strategies, and physical exercise will all need to improve. The nutrition plan, on the other hand, is one of the most important components of this journey.

A bariatric diet is one that is low in carbohydrates, high in protein, and low in sugar. You prioritize eating healthful foods and proteins and limit snacking between meals. To get you started, here's a six-week plan:

- **Week 1:** Maintain a liquid diet.
- **Week 2:** A liquid diet is strictly adhered to.
- **Week 3:** A pureed diet is introduced.
- **Weeks 4 and 5:** Diet that is soft/adaptable.
- In weeks 6 and beyond, follow a stabilization diet.

Bariatric eating is a healthy nutritional regimen for everyone, not just those who have had bariatric surgery recently.

Before beginning a diet, always consult with your primary care physician.

A bariatric diet may be beneficial if you have recently had bariatric surgery or wish to lose weight in a healthy and balanced manner. A bariatric diet will help you avoid foods high in trans-fat, processed foods, and between-meal snacking. This long-term diet focuses on protein-rich lean meats, low-fat dairy products, healthy grains with reduced fat, and plenty of fruits and vegetables. Maintaining the recovery time of the diet will help you stay healthy and fit for the rest of your life.

1.2 Health Advantages of a Bariatric Diet

A bariatric diet has numerous long-term health benefits.

One of the most significant advantages of a bariatric diet is that it lowers the risk of obesity-related disorders like:

- Diabetes type 2
- Stroke
- High cholesterol levels (hyperlipidemia)
- Blood pressure that is too high (hypertension)
- Heart disease
- Bone loss
- Anemia
- Some cancers
- Fatty liver disease

Other advantages of the bariatric diet include the following.

- In contrast to being morbidly obese, the risk of health harm can be lowered by decreasing and keeping weight after surgery using a bariatric diet.
- Weight loss with a bariatric diet will exacerbate the physical and mental health issues associated with obesity.
- A bariatric diet can help you look and feel better while also allowing you to live a healthier lifestyle.
- Your energy levels will rise, making it easier to go around and improving your overall quality of life.
- Correctly following a bariatric diet will boost your self-esteem and self-worth. It can provide you with a renewed sense of self-assurance, positive emotions, and control over a life that has long struggled with being overweight.

1.3 Foods to Consume and Foods to Avoid:

To help you reintroduce solid foods, a bariatric diet usually takes a step-by-step approach. The ease with which your body completely heals and then adjusts to diverse eating habits determines how quickly you go from one level to the next. After three months, you will be allowed to resume your normal eating habits.

You must be watchful at all times on the bariatric diet to:

- Consume 64 ounces of drink per day to prevent dehydration.

- Drink fluids between meals instead of with them. Wait thirty minutes after finishing a meal before drinking anything and thirty minutes before commencing a meal before drinking anything.

- Slowly drink and eat to prevent dumping syndrome. Dumping syndrome occurs when liquids and foods enter the small intestine at a faster and greater rate than usual, causing vomiting, nausea, sweating, disorientation, and diarrhea.

- Consume lean, nutritious foods on a regular basis.

- Pick foods and beverages that are low in fat and sugar.

- Stop drinking alcoholic beverages.

- Caffeine dehydrates you, so limit your intake.

- Take mineral and vitamin supplements on a regular basis, as directed by your healthcare professional.

- When you've progressed beyond only liquids, chew things until they're pureed before swallowing.

Let's look at some items you can consume and avoid while on a bariatric diet.

Pureed foods

After roughly a week of adjusting to liquids, those on a bariatric diet can start consuming strained & pureed (mashed up) foods. There should be no solid particles of food in the combination, and it should be the viscosity of a thick liquid or a smooth paste.

Three to six modest meals each day are sufficient. At each meal, 4 to 6 tablespoons of food should be consumed. Each meal should last approximately 30 minutes.

Select foods that are simple to puree, such as:

- Poultry, lean ground meat, or fish
- Soft-textured scrambled eggs
- Cottage cheese
- Cooked cereal
- Vegetables and soft fruits that have been cooked
- Cream soups that are strained
- Mix solid foods with liquids such as water.
- Juice that has not been sweetened
- Skimmed milk

- Boiling water

Soft Foods

With your doctor's clearance, you should add soft meals to your diet after a couple of weeks of consuming only pureed foods. Food portions must be thin, soft, and easy to chew.

3 to 5 small meals each day are sufficient. Each meal should consist of 1/3 to 1/2 cup of food. Chew each piece till it achieves a pureed consistency before swallowing.

Soft foods consist of the following:

- Ground poultry or ground meat
- Eggs
- Fish with flaked skin
- The cottage cheese
- Cereal, either dried or cooked
- Vegetables cooked without the skin
- Soft fresh fruit seedless or peeled, as well as canned fruit
- Rice

Solid Foods

After about 8 weeks on the bariatric diet, you will be capable to eat firmer foods again. Begin by eating three meals every day, each of which should contain about 1 to 1-1/2 food cups. It is critical to complete your meal before your stomach is full.

Depending on how well you handle solid food, you will be capable to change the total number of meals as well as the amount of food at each meal. Consult your dietician to find out what is best for you.

Try new meals one at a time. Some meals might induce discomfort, vomiting, or nausea after bariatric surgery.

At this point, the following foods may cause problems:

- Bread
- Raw vegetables
- Carbonated beverages
- Celery, broccoli, maize, cabbage, and other fibrous vegetables
- Foods that are fried

- Meats with a lot of marrow or that are difficult
- Popcorn
- Foods that have a lot of flavors or are spicy
- Nuts and seeds
- Red meat

With your doctor's approval, you may eventually be able to try any of the foods listed.

While on a bariatric diet, you should be able to resume your normal eating habits 4 months after surgery.

Foods to Avoid Include:

Certain foods increase the risk of problems after bariatric surgery and other bariatric procedures. As a result, patients on a bariatric diet should avoid such foods and beverages to reduce their chances of having an adverse event.

These foods and beverages include:

- Hard and dry foods, for example, are difficult to swallow following bariatric surgery.
- Foods and beverages high in calories.
- High glycemic index foods can cause blood sugar levels to surge quickly.
- Beans and chewing gum are examples of foods that cause flatulence.
- Food that has been microwaved.
- Foods high in fat and sugar.

1.4 Suggestions for Getting Started

Weight loss requires lifestyle changes such as healthy food and regular exercise. To begin a bariatric diet, you must first take certain critical actions.

Here are a few things you can do to get started on your bariatric diet:

Begin recording your food and water consumption:

Keeping track of your eating and drinking habits will provide you with vital information and put you on the proper path to growth.

Drink more water and limit your intake of other beverages:

Keep a close eye on your body's thirst indications. Adults need at least 64 ounces of water every day. Limit or eliminate liquid calorie sources such as beer, soda, juice, energy drinks, and coffee with cream or sugar. Caffeinated and carbonated beverages should be avoided. Avoid drinking liquids with meals and wait 30 minutes afterward before drinking.

Eat your meals in the sequence listed below:

1. Begin with protein

Eating the protein portion of your meal first makes it easier to receive adequate protein. Even if you're too full to finish the entire meal. Your body needs 60 to 80 grams of protein per day. Because you are only taking a limited amount of food, it is critical that you consume half (50%) of your regular meal as protein. Protein should be included in every meal and snack.

Keep track of what you eat in a diet record. Aim for 60 to 80 grams of protein per day.

2. Food and vegetables

3. Starch and grain.

Give yourself some breathing room:

Set aside 30 to 45 minutes for each meal. Chew your food 20 to 30 times per bite and place your fork down between bites. Delay, don't be alarmed, and enjoy your dinner.

Should you finish everything on your plate?

No, it is not required. Although getting adequate protein in your diet is vital, that doesn't mean you should force yourself to eat when you're already full. Listen to your hunger and fullness signals to notify your body when it's time to stop eating.

Taking small bites of food:

Make sure the food is cut into little bits. Smaller dishes and bowls may make it easier to control your portion proportions.

1 to 2 snacks and 3 meals per day are advised:

Grazing is not a good idea. Simply eat at a set meal or snack hour. Picking at food or grazing between meals might impede weight loss and prevent you from reaching your goal.

Have fun with your meal:

Slowly chew your food and relish the flavor. Make mindful eating a regular practice.

Obtain the help of your friends and family:

Explain to them why you need to eat slowly, so they don't put you under pressure to do so.

Make each bite count:

Because you won't be eating much, make every bite count. Choose the healthiest and most nutritious foods possible.

Following these few steps will make it easier for you to begin the bariatric diet.

1.5 Making the Most of Your Post-Surgery Life

Bariatric surgery reduces the size of your stomach to approximately 15% of its original size. Because your stomach can only hold 2-3 ounces following the operation, you may be able to eat less and still feel content. You will also have fewer hunger pangs.

To be effective for the bariatric surgery, you must commit to a new lifestyle and eating approach. Certain practices can assist you in adjusting to your new digestive environment and maintaining your weight loss following surgery. If you adopt the right behaviors, you can lose 60-70 percent of your excess weight in a year.

Consume nutrient-dense foods

You won't have much room in your stomach following surgery, so don't cram it with empty calories. Meals should include whole foods, including fresh fruit, vegetables, and protein. Processed foods, such as frozen or canned meals, should be utilized only as a last resort if fresh alternatives are available.

Fresh, whole meals keep you satiated for longer while also providing a variety of minerals, vitamins, and other nutrients. If you're used to eating less nutritious meals, whole foods may take a bit longer to prepare. Allow yourself some time to acclimate; it may take up to 20 attempts to adapt to and enjoy a dish.

Protein, protein, protein, and more protein

Protein should be included in every meal and snack. It keeps you feeling fuller for longer and helps you maintain muscle mass while shedding weight. When you sit down to a meal, eat the protein first if you become too full to finish everything on your plate.

Make a meal plan

Keep the ingredients for nutritious meals on hand, and prepare ahead of time what you'll eat when the time comes. When you dig through your refrigerator and pantry, you are more likely to give in and eat processed meals.

Consume no calories from beverages

You're on a liquid diet for the first few weeks after surgery. During this time, though, you must limit your consumption of calorie-dense beverages. Sugary coffee drinks, soda, juice, and sports drinks all increase your calorie intake while supplying you with the majority of the nutrients you require.

Chew slowly and thoroughly

Although you are consuming less calories, your stomach can only hold so much. Weight-loss surgery frequently causes nausea and vomiting. By chewing your food properly, you can avoid these unpleasant side effects. Large chunks of food may cause pain since they do not easily pass through your digestive tract.

Exercise

Start exercising as soon as your doctor says you can. Walking for 5-10 minutes at a time, several times a day, is a reasonable option, especially if longer periods feel daunting. Your stamina quickly improves.

Walking can help you prevent major difficulties, especially if you begin it soon after your surgery. In general, exercise can help you lose weight faster. Over time, it does make us feel better.

Never be frightened to seek assistance

This method necessitates major dietary and behavioral changes on the part of the patient. That is why it is difficult to keep up with everything on your own.

Ask for assistance during your recuperation, and don't be hesitant to seek advice from support groups or family members and friends who are aware of your condition after that.

Keep a positive attitude

Change is challenging and time-consuming. In life, patience and perseverance go a long way. You'll be well on your way to achieving your goal in no time.

1.6 Foods to Avoid and Final Recommendations

Some foods increase the risk of problems after bariatric surgery. As a result, some meals and beverages should be avoided to reduce the likelihood of an adverse event.

This list includes the following foods and beverages:

- Difficult-to-swallow meals following surgery, such as hard and dry foods
- High-calorie meals and beverages, such as chocolate, ice cream, cakes, and milkshakes
- Soda and other carbonated and sugary beverages
- Rice, bread, and potatoes have a high glycemic index, which causes blood sugar levels to spike quickly.
- Flatulence-causing foods, such as beans and chewing gum
- We strongly advise you not to consume any alcoholic beverages. Alcohol is taken much more rapidly into your system after surgery, adding to the difficulty of foreseeing and managing sedative and mood-altering effects.
- Avoid sugar, concentrated sweets, sugar-sweetened beverages and meals, and fruit juices.

Final Tips:

- Take a rest when you're exhausted. If you get enough sleep, you will be able to recover faster.

- Try to go for a walk every day. Begin by taking a longer walk than you did the day before. Increase your walking time gradually. Walking increases blood circulation and helps to prevent pneumonia and constipation.

- Lifting anything that creates strain is not recommended. This includes large grocery bags and milk containers, cat litter or dog food bags, a big briefcase or backpack, a vacuum cleaner, or a child.

- Avoid intense activity such as bicycling, jogging, lifting weights, or aerobic exercise unless your doctor says it's okay. Do not engage in any activity that could result in you becoming trapped in your stomach. Athletics and playing with children are instances of this.

- If you cough or take deep breaths, place a cushion above your incision to support your stomach and minimize discomfort.

- For at-home breathing exercises, follow your doctor's instructions. This will help with pneumonia prevention.

- You may now shower. With a paper towel, pat dry the wound. Do not take a bath for the first two weeks or until your doctor advises it is safe.

- You may drive if you are no longer taking prescription painkillers and can quickly transfer your foot from the accelerator to the brake pedal. Even if you do not want to travel far, you must be able to sit comfortably for an extended period of time. You might be stuck in traffic.

- You'll probably need to take two to four weeks off from work. It depends on the type of work you do and how you feel at the time.

- Following the operation, your doctor or dietitian will give you specific instructions on what to eat. For the first 14 days, you must follow a liquid diet. You will be able to gradually reintroduce solid foods into your diet.

- Speak with the dietitian on your bariatric surgery healthcare team about how to transition from a liquid to a solid diet and what will work best for you.

- When introducing solid meals, start with a small amount of soft solid food at a time (around 2-3 nibbles).

- Consume small amounts of food at least four times every day. You may need to eat 5 to 6 times a day if you aren't eating enough.

- At first, you may discover that you handle softer, wetter meals better. Some examples are eggs, salmon, mashed potatoes, cottage cheese, and soft, fresh fruit (peeled).

- Try one new food at a time. If a food causes indigestion, make a note of it in your journal and try it again later. Continue to eat the meals that are beneficial to you.

- Certain foods may cause discomfort after surgery because they are difficult to chew effectively. Meals that are tough, sticky, chewy, stringy, or gummy, for example. It's likely that your tolerance to different foods will change over time.

- Separate the liquids from the solid foods. It is not a good idea to drink with snacks and meals. Wait 30 minutes after eating a substantial meal before drinking. Between meals, drink lots of water.

- No straws should be used to drink. This may help you swallow less air when you drink.

- Consult your doctor before consuming alcohol. Your body may digest alcohol more quickly after surgery.

- Consult your healthcare professional if you are concerned about your bowel movements or constipation.

- Your doctor will tell you when and if you can start taking your meds again. She or he will also give you instructions on how to take any new medications.

- If you're taking aspirin or another blood thinner, consult your doctor about whether you should continue taking it. Make certain that you fully understand what your doctor is asking you to do.

- If your doctor has prescribed pain medication, take it exactly as prescribed.

- Do not take two or more pain medicines simultaneously unless your doctor instructs you to. Acetaminophen, widely known as Tylenol, is used in various pain medications. Excessive use of acetaminophen (Tylenol) may be hazardous.

- Do not take aspirin (Asaphen, Entrophen), ibuprofen (Advil, Motrin), or naproxen (Aleve) until your doctor approves.

- If you believe your pain medicine is causing you to become ill, take the following steps:

- Take your medication after each meal.

- Ask your doctor for an alternative pain reliever.

- If your doctor has prescribed antibiotics, please follow the instructions. You shouldn't stop taking them just because you're feeling better. You must finish the entire antibiotic course.

- Aftercare for surgical incisions. If there are tape strips on the incision, leave them on for a week or until they come off.

- Regularly wash the area with warm soapy water and wipe it dry. Avoid using hydrogen peroxide or alcohol since they may inhibit the healing process. If the wound is bleeding or rubbing against clothing, apply a gauze bandage. The bandage should be changed daily.

1.7 What is the Air fryer?

The counter space is a valuable asset in practically every kitchen. And if you have a lot of it, it's tempting to overcrowd it with the latest culinary devices. You will, however, need to make room for an air fryer. To achieve the same fried texture as a deep fryer, but without the oil, you can use an air fryer, which is a little convection oven that fits on your countertop.

The top of an air fryer houses a heating element and a fan. Hot air flows down and around the food when you turn on the fryer. Because of the quick circulation, the food becomes crisp, similar to deep-frying but without the oil. Depending on the size of your air fryer, the air fryer basket can hold anything from two to ten quarts. Typically, 1 to 2 teaspoons of oil are required to allow the meal to become crispy. Air fryer cooking temperatures and periods range from 5 to 25 minutes at 350° to 400°F, depending on the food. To ensure that the food crisps up evenly, flip or change it halfway through cooking. After you've completed cooking, you must clean the air fryer.

In recent years, the air fryer has grown in popularity. According to NPD Group, a market research firm, around 40% of US houses had one as of July 2020. Air-frying can be used to cook everything from frozen chicken wings and handmade French fries to roasted vegetables and fresh-baked cookies.

1.8 Advantages of Air Frying

When you bite into a dish of French fries or a piece of fried chicken, you immediately notice the classic crispy crunch and juicy, chewy core.

The exquisite taste of fried dishes, however, comes at a cost. The oils used to prepare them, according to the study, are linked to health risks such as type 2 diabetes, cancer, and heart disease.

With air frying, you may enjoy the taste, texture, and golden-brown color of oil-fried items without the fat and calories.

There are numerous advantages to air frying.

- Consumption of fried foods is directly connected to an increased risk of obesity. This is because deep-fried foods have high fat and calorie content. Weight loss can be aided by switching from deep-fried to air-fried foods and limiting daily consumption of harmful oils.

- The most prevalent source of acrylamide generation is high-temperature cooking, such as frying, roasting, or baking. This substance is carcinogenic and increases the incidence of ovarian, pancreatic, endometrial, breast, and esophageal cancers. However, air frying may assist in decreasing this danger.

- Food cooks faster in an air fryer than in a tiny toaster oven or a large household oven. Baking potatoes or roasting Brussels sprouts in an air fryer takes about half the time and consumes significantly less energy due to the smaller size and power requirements. While air frying isn't as rapid as microwave cooking, it won't make your reheated fries or bread mushy, and it's an easy method to master.

- This is probably our favorite part of air frying. There is so much you can do with it! Yes, it fries incredibly nicely in comparison to an oven. It can, however, bake (even cakes), stir fry, roast, broil, and barbecue! Do you like a supper of chicken and snow peas? It's simple to create with any of these.

- You may use an air fryer for cooking both frozen and fresh dishes, as well as to reheat leftovers. Meats, fish, sandwiches, casseroles, and various veggies are available. In certain fryers, a grill pan, rotisserie rack, or elevated frying rack is employed. Because the baskets may be divided, you can prepare multiple recipes simultaneously. Surprisingly, a single device can cook almost a variety of items in various ways.

- Simply set the air fryer temperature and cooking time, add the food, and shake the air fryer many times during cooking. There's no need to much around or stir like you would on a stove. Air fryer baskets make tossing your food simple and quick, and the gadget doesn't lose much heat when opened, so go ahead and peek into the kitchen while it's cooking! If you do this, you will not be slowing things down as you would in an oven.

- One component of cooking that many of us dread is the cleanup. You only need to clean an air fryer's pan and basket when air frying, and some are dishwasher safe. Food does not attach to the nonstick-coated portions of the pan and instead falls directly onto the plate. Cleaning up the air fryer after air frying will just take a few minutes.

- Air frying is ideal for folks who dislike cooking. There's no need to waste time defrosting, preparing ingredients, or putting together meals. It's great for frozen chicken wings, ribeye steaks, and even frozen pizza. Fries, onion rings, potato tots, and nuggets may all be prepared in a matter of minutes. A package of pre-cut vegetables can be used to make a quick stir fry. Do you enjoy grilled cheese sandwiches? Make it yourself.

1.9 Cleaning your Air Fryer

Do you know how to clean an air fryer? It's a lot simpler than you think!

You'll have grease to clean up if you use an air fryer. What exactly is the good news? Because it's an air fryer, you'll have a far less greasy mess to clean than a deep fryer. Learn how to clean an air fryer with household items you most likely already have.

Before you begin deep cleaning your air fryer, review the dos and don'ts of air fryer maintenance.

- Avoid using metal tools, steel wire brushes, or abrasive sponges to remove residue and food particles from your air fryer. As a result, the nonstick coating on your air fryer may be destroyed.

- Avoid immersing the air fryer in water. Because an air fryer is an electric appliance, this can cause it to malfunction.

- If your air fryer has a bad odor, add half a lemon to the basket and set it away for 30 minutes before cleaning.

How often should you clean your air fryer?

Following Each Use:

Use the soap every single time, you use your air fryer, wash the basket, pan, and tray with hot water or set them in the dishwasher. (Check the owner's handbook to ensure that these items are dishwasher safe.) Make a fast cleaning of the interior with a moist cloth and a small bit of dish soap. After all of the pieces have dried, reassemble them.

After a Few Uses:

Though these steps aren't required after every usage, doing them frequently will keep your air fryer in good working order. Wipe the device's exterior with a moist cloth regularly. You should also look for any oil or residue on the heating coil. Allow the machine to cool before cleaning it down with a moist cloth if there is any build-up.

Learn how to thoroughly clean an air fryer

If you haven't cleaned your air fryer in a while or aren't sure where to start, stay reading for step-by-step instructions on how to clean an air fryer.

Here's a checklist of what you'll need to get started:

- A non-abrasive sponge or damp microfiber cloth
- Gentle bristle scrub brush
- Dishwashing detergent
- Baking powder
- A clean, dry cloth

Directions:

- To begin, disconnect the air fryer and allow it to cool for around 30 minutes.
- Remove the air fryer's pans and baskets and wash them using hot, soapy water. If any of these parts have baked-on grease or food, immerse them in soapy hot water for at least 10 minutes before washing them with a sponge. Some of the components may be dishwasher friendly; if you decide to use the dishwasher, examine your owner's manual.
- Wipe the interior down with a nonabrasive sponge or a wet microfiber towel dampened with dish soap. Wipe away the soap with a clean, moist cloth.
- Invert the air fryer and clean the heating element with a moist cloth or sponge.

- If you notice some stubborn residue, baked-on, or substance on the primary device, make a paste of water and baking soda. Scrub the paste all over the residue with a soft-bristle scrub brush, then wipe it down with a clean cloth.

- Wipe the appliance's outside using a moist towel. Wipe away the soap with a clean, moist cloth.

- Ensure that the main device and all removable pieces are totally dry before reassembling.

- Let's get to the recipes now that you've learned everything there is to know about the bariatric diet and air fryer. In the next chapters, you will learn how to create a variety of tasty bariatric diet dishes in an air fryer.

Chapter 2: Breakfast Recipes

1. Scrambled Breakfast Eggs

Preparation time: 10 minutes
Cooking time: 15 minutes
Servings: 2
Nutrition facts (Per serving) Calories 359 Total Fat 27.6g Protein 19.5g Carbs 1.1g
Ingredients:
- 1/2 teaspoon of vegetable oil
- Salt and pepper according to taste
- 4 eggs large
- 1/2 cup of sharp Parmesan cheese grated

Instructions:
- In a 2-cup round baking pan, crack and whisk the eggs. Place the dish in the air fryer basket.
- Set the air fryer timer for 10 minutes and cook at 390°F.
- Stir in the butter and cheese halfway through the cooking time.
- Remove the eggs from the air fryer and fluff them with a fork. Season using salt and pepper and serve warm.

2. Tasty Breakfast Eggplant Pizza

Preparation time: 10 minutes
Cooking time: 20 minutes
Servings: 8
Nutrition facts (Per serving): Calories 80, Total Fat 6g, Protein 3g, Carbs 4g
Ingredients:
- 1 eggplant
- 3/4 cup of mozzarella cheese grated
- 2 tablespoons of olive oil
- 1/2 cup of tomato sauce

Instructions:
- Preheat the air fryer at 390°F and spray the air fryer basket using cooking spray.
- Cut eggplant into thin slices and drizzle with olive oil. Place the slices in your fryer basket, not overlapping them. Cook for 10 minutes in the air fryer, then flip the eggplant over and cook for another 3 minutes.
- Spread the tomato sauce over the eggplant slices and top with your favorite cheese and garnishes. Air-fried for another 2 to 3 minutes or till the eggplants begin to brown and the cheese melts.

3. Classic Air Fried Breakfast Frittata

Preparation time: 10 minutes
Cooking time: 30 minutes
Servings: 2
Nutrition facts (Per serving) Calories 380 Total fat 27.4g Protein 31.2g Carbs 2.9g
Ingredients:
- 1/2 cup of Cheddar-Monterey Jack cheese blend shredded
- 4 lightly beaten eggs
- 1/4 pound of crumbled and fully cooked breakfast sausage
- 1 chopped green onion
- 2 tablespoons of diced red bell pepper
- Cooking spray
- 1 pinch of cayenne pepper (Optional)

Instructions:
- Combine the Cheddar-Monterey jack cheese, bell pepper, eggs, sausage, cayenne pepper, and onion inside a medium-sized mixing bowl. Mix them thoroughly till completely mixed.
- Set your air fryer at 360°F.
- Coat a 6x2 inch cake pan using nonstick cooking spray.
- Spread the egg mixture evenly in the nonstick cake pan.
- In the air fryer, cook for around 18 to 20 minutes or till the frittata is set.

4. Avocado Cauliflower Toast

Preparation time: 10 minutes
Cooking time: 20 minutes
Servings: 2
Nutrition facts (Per serving) Calories 278 Total fat 15.6g Protein 14.1g Carbs 7.7g
Ingredients:
- 12 oz. of steamer bag cauliflower
- 1 cup of cheddar cheese shredded
- 1/4 teaspoon of black pepper
- 1 egg large
- 1/2 teaspoon of garlic powder
- 1 avocado ripe

Instructions:
- Cook cauliflower according to package directions, then drain excess moisture using a kitchen cloth or cheesecloth.
- Inside a large-sized mixing dish, combine the cheddar, cauliflower, and egg. Line the air fryer basket using parchment paper. Divide the cauliflower mixture in half and shape it into two mounds on baking paper. Press the mounds together to form a 1/4-inch-thick rectangle. Place them in an air fryer basket that has been lined.
- Cook for 8 minutes at 390°F in the air fryer.
- After 4 minutes, rotate the cauliflower and cook for another 4 minutes. Allow it cool for a few minutes after cooking.
- Remove the pit from the avocado, scoop out the center, and mash well with pepper and garlic powder inside a medium-sized bowl. Serve with the cauliflower spread.

5. Air Fried Cheesy Egg Bites

Preparation time: 10 minutes
Cooking time: 15 minutes
Servings: 4
Nutrition facts (Per serving) Calories 195 Total fat 15g Protein 10g Carbs 3g
Ingredients:
- 1/2 small diced bell pepper
- 4 eggs
- 1/4 cup of shredded cheese of your choice
- Salt and pepper according to taste
- 4 strips of cooked and crumbled bacon
- 1/2 diced onion
- 4 teaspoons of milk

Instructions:
- Place four silicone muffin cups in your air fryer basket. Pour 1 teaspoon of milk into each cup and crack 1 egg into each.
- Sprinkle green pepper, sliced onions, bacon bits, and cheese into each cup. Season using salt and pepper to taste.
- At 300°F, air fry for around 10 to 13 minutes.

6. Air Fryer Breakfast Apple Protein Muffins

Preparation time: 10 minutes
Cooking time: 25 minutes
Servings: 12
Nutrition facts (Per serving) Calories 76 Fat 1g Protein 3g Carbs 15g
Ingredients:
- 2 teaspoons of cinnamon
- 4 egg whites
- 2 cups of rolled oats
- 1 diced apple
- 2 tablespoons of sugar substitute
- 1/2 teaspoon of baking powder
- 2 scoops of vanilla protein powder
- 1 cup of Greek yogurt non-fat
- 2 scoops of vanilla protein powder
- Pinch of kosher salt

Instructions:
- Preheat your air fryer at 350°F and cover the ramekins using cooking spray.
- Combine all of the ingredients inside a large-sized mixing bowl and stir thoroughly. After everything has been combined, distribute evenly between ramekins.
- Place the ramekins in the air fryer basket. If necessary, cook in batches to avoid them touching.
- Cook for approximately 15-20 minutes. Allow it cool for a few minutes before serving.

7. Chanterelle Mushrooms and Zucchini Omelet

Preparation time: 10 minutes
Cooking time: 15 minutes
Servings: 1
Nutrition facts (Per serving) Calories 264 Total Fat 20.4g Protein 13.3g Carbs 6.7g
Ingredients:
- 2 eggs medium
- 1 finely chopped garlic clove
- 1/3 thinly sliced zucchini
- 4 thinly sliced chanterelle mushrooms
- Salt and pepper to taste
- 1/4 cup of mozzarella cheese shredded
- 1 tablespoon of butter

Instructions:
- Melt butter in a nonstick skillet over a high flame. Cook and stir garlic for 2 to 3 minutes or till crispy and golden brown. Reduce the flame to medium. At this point, add the zucchini and chanterelle mushrooms. For 5 minutes, or till golden brown, cook and stir.
- Whisk together the egg, pepper, and salt in a medium-sized mixing dish.
- Spray a circular cake pan using nonstick cooking spray. Spread the egg mixture on the bottom of the pan and push down the cooked zucchini and mushroom. On top, sprinkle with cheese.
- Place pan in air fryer basket and cook for around 10 to 15 minutes at 370°F.

8. Breakfast Portobello Pizzas

Preparation time: 10 minutes
Cooking time: 13 minutes
Servings: 6
Nutrition facts (Per serving) Calories 317 Total Fat 26.1g Protein 14.9g Carbs 5.5g
Ingredients:
- 2 tablespoons of extra virgin olive oil
- 6 thinly sliced cherry or grape tomatoes
- 1 1/2 cups of shredded mozzarella cheese reduced-fat
- 6 teaspoons of Italian seasoning
- Salt and pepper, according to taste
- 30 pepperonis miniature-sized
- 6 caps of Portobello mushroom, washed, stems removed and dried using a paper towel
- 3/4 cup of pizza sauce (garlic and herb)
- 2 teaspoons of garlic minced

Instructions:
- Inside a small-sized mixing bowl, combine the garlic, oil, and 4 teaspoons of Italian seasoning. Apply the garlic oil mixture on the bottoms of all mushrooms.
- Stuff each mushroom cap with 2 tablespoons of pizza sauce, 6 pepperoni miniatures, tomato slices, and 1/4 cup of mozzarella.
- Cook the Portobello mushrooms in an air fryer for 8 minutes at 370°F or till the cheese melts.
- When serving, top with remaining seasoning and season using salt and pepper to taste.

9. Cheesy Cauliflower Hash Browns

Preparation time: 10 minutes
Cooking time: 30 minutes
Servings: 4
Nutrition facts (Per serving) Calories 153 Total Fat 9.5g Protein 10.0g Carbs 3.0g
Ingredients:
- 1 egg large
- 12 oz. of steamer bag cauliflower
- 1 cup of sharp Parmesan cheese shredded

Instructions:
- Place a cauliflower bag in the microwave and cook according to the package guidelines. Allow it to cool before placing it in a kitchen cloth or cheesecloth. Squeeze thoroughly to eliminate any moisture.
- Mash cauliflower using a fork and stir in cheese and egg.
- Line the basket of your air fryer using parchment paper. Make a hash brown patty out of 1/4 of the mixture and place it in the air fryer basket coated with parchment paper. Work in groups.

- Cook for 12 minutes at 390°F in an air fryer. Flip the hash browns halfway through the cooking time. Cook till golden brown and crispy. Serve immediately.

10. Breakfast Feta and Spinach Casserole

Preparation time: 10 minutes
Cooking time: 30 minutes
Servings: 4
Nutrition facts (Per serving) Calories 211 Total fat 13.4g Protein 14.8g Carbs 9.3g
Ingredients:
- 1 clove of minced garlic
- 1/4 cup of feta cheese crumbled
- 2 beaten eggs
- 1 can of drained and squeezed spinach (13.5 ounces)
- 2 tablespoons of melted butter
- 1 cup of cottage cheese
- 2 tablespoons of almond flour
- 1 1/2 teaspoons of onion powder
- 1/8 teaspoon of ground nutmeg
- Cooking spray

Instructions:
- Grease an 8-inch baking pan using cooking spray and warm your air fryer to 375°F.
- Inside a medium-sized mixing bowl, combine cottage cheese, feta cheese, spinach, eggs, butter, garlic, onion powder, flour, and nutmeg. Stir till completely combined. Fill a greased pie pan halfway with the mixture.
- Air fry for around 18 to 20 minutes or till completely set.

11. Healthy and Crunchy Breakfast Granola

Preparation time: 10 minutes
Cooking time: 15 minutes
Servings: 6
Nutrition facts (Per serving) Calories 617 Total fat 55.8g Protein 10.9g Carbs 6.5g
Ingredients:
- 1/3 cup of sunflower seeds
- 1/4 cup of chopped Brazil Nuts
- 1 cup of almond slivers
- 2 cups of chopped pecans
- 1/4 cup of golden flaxseed
- 1 cup of coconut flakes unsweetened
- 2 tablespoons of butter unsalted
- 1/4 cup of chocolate chips sugar-free and low carb
- 1 teaspoon of cinnamon
- 1/4 cup of granular erythritol

Instructions:
- Inside a medium-sized mixing bowl, combine all of the ingredients indicated above.
- Pour the mixture into a 4-cup round baking dish and place it in an air fryer basket.
- Cook for 5 to 10 minutes in an air fryer set at 320°F.
- Allow cooling completely before serving. Stir well and serve.

12. Creamy Veggie Breakfast Frittata

Preparation time: 10 minutes
Cooking time: 20 minutes
Servings: 4
Nutrition facts (Per serving) Calories 168 Total fat 11.8g Protein 10.2g Carbs 2.5g
Ingredients:
- 1/2 cup of grape tomatoes
- 1/4 cup of heavy whipping cream
- 6 eggs large
- 1/4 cup of yellow onion chopped
- 1/2 cup of spinach chopped
- Salt and pepper according to taste
- 1/2 cup of broccoli chopped
- 1/4 cup of green bell pepper chopped

Instructions:
- Inside a large-sized mixing dish, combine heavy whipping cream and eggs. Incorporate the onion, bell pepper, spinach, tomatoes, and broccoli.
- Spread the mixture onto a 6-inch round oven-safe baking dish and place it in the air fryer basket.
- Cook for around 12 to 15 minutes at 350°F in an air fryer.

13. Cheese, Egg and Bacon Roll-Ups

Preparation time: 10 minutes
Cooking time: 30 minutes
Servings: 4
Nutrition facts (Per serving) Calories 460 Total fat 31.7g Protein 28.2g Carbs 5.3g
Ingredients:
- 1/2 chopped and seeded green bell pepper
- 12 bacon
- 2 tablespoons of butter unsalted
- 1/4 cup of onion chopped
- 6 eggs large
- 1 cup of sharp Parmesan cheese shredded

Instructions:
- Inside a medium-sized skillet over medium flame, melt the butter. Cook for about 3 minutes, till the pepper and onion is transparent.
- Scramble the eggs inside a small bowl and set in a skillet with the peppers and onions. Remove from the flame and put aside.
- On a kitchen-floured surface, place three bacon pieces' side by side, 1/4 inch apart. Spread 1/4 cup of scrambled eggs on one side and top with 1/4 cup of cheese.
- Roll the bacon tightly around the eggs, inserting toothpicks to tighten the seam if necessary. Place the rolls in the air fryer basket.
- Cook for about 15 minutes at 350°F in an air fryer. Flip the rolls halfway through cooking. Serve immediately.

14. Crustless Breakfast Quiche

Preparation time: 10 minutes
Cooking time: 30 minutes
Servings: 6
Nutrition facts (Per serving) Calories 216 Total fat 17g Protein 11g Carbs 4g
Ingredients:
- 1/2 cup of milk
- 5 eggs
- 1/2 cup of chopped bacon
- 1/2 teaspoon of salt
- 1/2 cup of half and half
- 2/3 cup of mozzarella cheese shredded
- 1/4 teaspoon of ground black pepper
- 1/2 cup of chopped cherry tomatoes
- 1/2 cup of chopped broccoli

Instructions:
- Set your air fryer at 320°F.
- Coat a baking dish using nonstick cooking spray. Arrange the broccoli, bacon, and tomato slices in an equal layer on the bottom of the baking dish.
- Whisk together the milk, salt, half and half, eggs, and pepper till creamy.
- In a baking pan, spread the egg mixture over the vegetables. Cheese should be sprinkled on top. Place the pan inside the air fryer basket.
- Cook for around 20 minutes in the air fryer. Allow the quiche to cool completely before serving.

15. Breakfast Mashed Potato Pancakes

Preparation time: 10 minutes
Cooking time: 20 minutes
Servings: 6
Nutrition facts (Per serving) Calories 12 Total fat 1g Protein 1g Carbs 3g
Ingredients:
- 1 teaspoon of oregano
- 3 diced green onions (white and green parts)
- 1/2 teaspoon of smoked paprika
- 2 tablespoons of gluten-free flour
- 2 1/3 cup of cold mashed potatoes leftover
- 1 egg

Instructions:
- Inside a medium-sized mixing dish, combine the mashed potatoes, green onions, flour, and spices. In a small-sized bowl, scramble an egg, then add it to the potato mixture.

- Combine all of the ingredients and form patties. Place the pancakes in the air fryer basket.
- Cook for around 10 to 12 minutes at 380°F in an air fryer.
- Flip the pancakes halfway through cooking.

16. Cheese and Ham Omelet

Preparation time: 10 minutes
Cooking time: 20 minutes
Servings: 6
Nutrition facts (Per serving) Calories 313 Total Fat 19.4g Protein 26.1g Carbs 7.3g
Ingredients:
- 1 teaspoon of salt
- 10 large-sized eggs
- 1 cup of ham cooked
- 1/4 cup of fresh leaf parsley chopped
- 2 cups of milk
- 1/2 teaspoon of black pepper
- 1 cup of shredded Parmesan cheese

Instructions:
- Coat a 6x3-inch baking dish lightly with olive oil or nonstick cooking spray.
- Inside a large-sized mixing dish, combine the eggs and milk. Combine the ham, cheese, and parsley in a mixing dish and season using salt and pepper (At this stage, cover the pan and refrigerate for up to 24 hours).
- Insert the pan into the air fryer basket. Cook for around 8-10 minutes at 350°F or till the eggs are cooked through. Serve immediately.

17. Low-Carb Air Fried Garlic Bread

Preparation time: 10 minutes
Cooking time: 35 minutes
Servings: 8
Nutrition facts (Per serving) Calories 283 Total Fat 25.8g Protein 10g Total Carbs 1.6g
Ingredients:
- 1 teaspoon of baking powder
- 3 eggs lightly beaten
- 2 tablespoons of psyllium husk
- 1 1/2 cups of almond meal
- 1 cup of mozzarella cheese grated
- 2 tablespoons of olive oil
- 1 tablespoon of pouring cream
- 1/3 cup of warm water
- 3 cloves of garlic
- 7g sachet of instant yeast
- 1 tablespoon of ground flaxseed
- 2 teaspoons of apple cider vinegar
- 1 teaspoon of baking powder
- Chopped parsley for serving
- 1/2 teaspoon of table salt

Instructions:
- Line a loaf pan using baking paper and grease it. In a small-sized cup, combine the yeast, cream, and water. To blend the ingredients, whisk them together. Set them aside for 10 minutes or till they bubble up.
- Combine the psyllium husk, almond meal, flaxseed, baking powder, and salt in a large-sized mixing dish. Make a well in the center. Combine the yeast mixture, olive oil, vinegar, and egg in a mixing dish. To blend, thoroughly whisk everything together. Spread the batter evenly in the prepared loaf pan. Set aside for 1 hour, or till the mixture has risen, covered loosely using plastic wrap.
- Cook the loaf pan in the air fryer basket for around 20 minutes at 380°F. In the midst of the cooking process, drizzle olive oil all over the bread, then season using garlic and cheese. Bake for another 10 minutes or till the cheese melts. When serving, sprinkle parsley on top of the garlic bread.

18. Sugar-Free Air fried Mix Berries Oatmeal

Preparation time: 10 minutes
Cooking time: 20 minutes
Servings: 6
Nutrition facts (Per serving) Calories 383 Total Fat 20g Protein 10g Total Carbs 4g
Ingredients:

- 1 3/4 cups of low-fat milk
- 1/2 teaspoon of nutmeg
- 2 cups of oats
- 1/3 cup of sugar-free maple syrup
- 3 tablespoons of butter unsalted
- 3/4 cup of chopped walnuts
- 1 teaspoon of cinnamon
- 2 eggs large
- 1 teaspoon of baking powder
- 1/2 teaspoon of salt
- 1 teaspoon of vanilla
- 2 cups of mixed berries
- Greek yogurt for serving

Instructions:
- Coat a 9x9-inch baking pan using cooking oil. Toast the walnuts in a skillet till fragrant, about four to five minutes. Remove the walnuts from the pan and carefully chop them.
- Inside a medium-sized mixing bowl, combine oats, nutmeg, walnuts, cinnamon, salt, and baking powder.
- Inside a separate small-sized mixing dish, combine the milk, eggs, maple syrup, butter, and vanilla extract. In a mixing dish, combine the ingredients, beginning with the oats. Fold in the berries, then distribute the mixture evenly in the baking dish.
- Place the baking dish in the air fryer basket and cook for around 8 to 10 minutes at 390°F or till the top is golden brown. On the side, serve with Greek yogurt.

19. Italian-Style Air Fried Breakfast Eggs

Preparation time: 10 minutes
Cooking time: 15 minutes
Servings: 4
Nutrition facts (Per serving) Calories 121 Total Fat 1.9g Protein 7.2g Total Carbs 1.4g
Ingredients:
- 4 teaspoons of extra virgin olive oil
- 4 teaspoons of basil fresh
- 1/4 teaspoon of black pepper ground
- 4 eggs large
- 10 sliced grape tomatoes
- 4 teaspoons of grated Parmigiano-Reggiano cheese
- 1/4 teaspoon of salt

Instructions:
- Grease four ramekins using 1 teaspoon of oil each, using a pastry brush.
- Fill each ramekin halfway with 5 to 6 tomato slices.
- Fill each ramekin with 1 teaspoon of basil.
- One egg at a time carefully breaks into each ramekin.
- Sprinkle 1 teaspoon of cheese, pepper, and salt into each ramekin.
- Cook the ramekins in the air fryer basket for around 10 to 15 minutes at 350°F.

20. Mushrooms and Taleggio Omelet

Preparation time: 10 minutes
Cooking time: 15 minutes
Servings: 2
Nutrition facts (Per serving) Calories 396 Total fat 31.4g Protein 27.1g Carbs 0.8g
Ingredients:
- 1 garlic clove crushed
- 50g of sliced taleggio cheese
- 2 eggs beaten and seasoned
- A handful of rocket leaves
- 150g of sliced chestnut mushrooms
- Butter for greasing

Instructions:
- Butter a 6x3-inch baking dish.
- Inside a mixing dish, combine all of the ingredients indicated above. Transfer the mixture to an air fryer basket after pouring it into a greased baking dish.
- Cook for around 10 to 15 minutes at 350°F in the air fryer or till the eggs is totally cooked. Serve immediately.

21. Cheesy Chicken, Carrot and Spinach Omelet

Preparation time: 10 minutes
Cooking time: 30 minutes
Servings: 6

Nutrition facts (Per serving) Calories 200 Total fat 10g Protein 19g Carbs 7g

Ingredients:
- 3 tablespoons of grated asiago cheese
- 4 cups of baby spinach
- 1/4 cup of plain yogurt
- 1/2 lb. of skinless and boneless chicken breasts
- 1 teaspoon of Dijon mustard
- 8 eggs medium
- 1 cup of sliced red onions
- 3 tablespoons of olive oil
- 1 cup of grated carrots
- 1/4 teaspoon of salt

Instructions:
- Cut chicken breasts into 1/2-inch pieces.
- Heat 1 teaspoon of olive oil inside a medium-sized pan and sauté chicken breasts with onions till brown and done about 10 minutes. Remove to a platter and pour the remaining olive oil into the pan.
- Whisk together the eggs, Dijon mustard, and salt till just combined. Place the egg mixture, prepared chicken, and onion in a baking dish and top with spinach and chopped carrot. Press the spinach down.
- Place the pan in an air fryer basket and cook at 350°F for about 20 minutes. Top with Asiago cheese and cut into 6 slices. Enjoy with a fresh green salad!

22. Crustless Breakfast Caprese Quiche

Preparation time: 10 minutes
Cooking time: 30 minutes
Servings: 6
Nutrition facts (Per serving) Calories 218 Total fat 14.6g Protein 17.4g Carbs 3.5g

Ingredients:
- 1/2 cup of chopped fresh basil
- 10 Eggs large
- 1 1/2 cups of halved grape tomatoes
- 1/2 cup of the almond milk unsweetened
- 6 oz. of mozzarella cheese fresh
- 1/4 teaspoon of black pepper
- 4 minced garlic cloves
- 3/4 teaspoon of sea salt

Instructions:
- Set your air fryer at 370°F.
- Combine the basil, tomatoes, garlic, and 2/3 of the mozzarella pieces inside a medium-sized mixing bowl. Spread the mixture in the bottom of a 9-inch glass or ceramic pan (round or square).
- Inside a mixing bowl, combine the eggs, milk, black pepper, and sea salt (you can reuse the same bowl). In the pan, layer the egg mixture over the tomatoes and basil.
- Cook for about 25 minutes in the air fryer; after 20 minutes, sprinkle the remaining mozzarella slices on top of the quiche. Cook till the cooking time is up.
- Before serving, drain any liquid at the dish's edges (from the tomatoes). Garnish using more basil leaves on top.

23. Air Fried Caprese Stuffed Avocado

Preparation time: 10 minutes
Cooking time: 20 minutes
Servings: 4
Nutrition facts (Per serving) Calories 191 Total fat 16g Protein 5g Carbs 10g

Ingredients:
- 2/3 cup of halved grape tomatoes
- 4 teaspoons of balsamic vinegar
- 2 California avocado large
- Black pepper
- 1/4 cup of fresh basil
- 2 oz. of mozzarella cheese (cut into small pieces)
- Sea salt

Instructions:
- Cut avocados in half and remove the pits. Remove half of the flesh from each avocado and leave the other half flashed.
- Mash the avocado flesh inside a medium-sized mixing bowl. Mix in the fresh mozzarella, grape tomatoes, and basil. Mix in the sea salt and black pepper.

- Return the mixture to the avocado halves and place in the air fryer basket.
- At 350°F, air fry for about 10 minutes.
- While serving, drizzle some balsamic vinegar.

24. Fluffy Air Fried Courgette Omelet

Preparation time: 10 minutes
Cooking time: 20 minutes
Servings: 1
Nutrition facts (Per serving) Calories 350 Total fat 27.6g Protein 21.1g Carbs 3.3g
Ingredients:
- 2 finely chopped spring onions
- 1 tablespoon of grated parmesan cheese
- Butter
- 2 eggs, separated
- 1 medium courgette grated
- Cooking spray
- Salt and pepper to taste

Instructions:
- Melt the butter in a medium-sized skillet over medium flame, then add the courgette and sauté for 3-4 minutes before adding the spring onion and sautéing for 1 minute. Remove from the flame and put aside.
- In one dish, whisk the egg yolks with 1 tablespoon of water, and in another, beat the egg whites with an electric mixer till frothy. Season the egg whites and yolks using pepper and salt.
- Cooking spray should be used to grease a round cake pan. Pour the eggs on the bottom and press down the sautéed courgette and spring onions. Top the eggs with parmesan cheese.
- Air fry for around 10 to 15 minutes at 350°F.
- Serve warm.

25. Classic Air fried Egg Casserole

Preparation time: 10 minutes
Cooking time: 20 minutes
Servings: 8
Nutrition facts (Per serving) Calories 374 Total fat 31.4g Protein 21g Carbs 2.2g
Ingredients:
- 1 tablespoon of onion minced
- 3/4 cup of heavy whipping cream
- 12 eggs
- 1 (8 ounces) package of Cheddar cheese shredded
- 2 teaspoons of dry mustard
- 1 (8 ounces) package of breakfast sausage
- Salt and pepper to taste
- 1 teaspoon of dried oregano

Instructions:
- Preheat the air fryer at 370°F.
- Cook sausage inside a large-sized skillet over medium flame, breaking it up with a spoon as it cooks, till crumbled and browned, around 5 to 10 minutes. Cover the bottom of a 9-inch casserole dish with the mixture.
- Whisk together the eggs, cream, mustard, oregano, salt, cheddar cheese, and pepper. Pour the sauce over the sausage.
- Air fry for around 20 minutes at 390°F.

26. Air Fryer Cheese Picante Omelet Pie

Preparation time: 10 minutes
Cooking time: 20 minutes
Servings: 6
Nutrition facts (Per serving) Calories 298 Total Fat 23g Protein 16g Carbs 4g
Ingredients:
- 1 cup shredded Monterey Jack cheese
- 1 cup of sour cream
- 1/2 cup of Picante sauce
- 6 eggs large
- 1 cup of cheddar cheese shredded

Instructions:
- Spread the Picante sauce on the bottom of a 9-inch greased pie pan. After distributing the cheeses on top of the Picante sauce layer, set the pie plate aside. In a blender, combine the sour cream and eggs and

blend till smooth. Pour the mixture over the Picante and cheese layer.
- Place the pie plate in the basket of the air fryer. Cook for around 10-15 minutes at 350°F or till the eggs are cooked through. Serve immediately.

27. Air Fryer Avocado Egg Boat

Preparation time: 10 minutes
Cooking time: 20 minutes
Servings: 2
Nutrition facts (Per serving) Calories 280 Total Fat 23.5g Protein 11.3g Carbs 9.3g
Ingredients:
- 2 teaspoons of chopped fresh chives
- 1 halved and pitted avocado
- 2 eggs medium
- Pinch of black pepper and sea salt
- 2 slices of cooked and crumbled bacon

Instructions:
- Preheat the air fryer at 390°F.
- Fill a small cup halfway with two eggs, being careful not to crack the yolks. Keep them together.
- On a baking sheet, place half of an avocado. Fill each half-avocado hole with 1 egg yolk. Fill the hole with egg white till it's completely full. Repeat with the remainder of the avocado. Each avocado should be topped with chives, salt, and pepper.
- For around 10-15 minutes, air fry. Serve and have fun!

28. Air Fried Sheet Pan Eggs

Preparation time: 10 minutes
Cooking time: 10 minutes
Servings: 12-15
Nutrition facts (Per serving) Calories 105 Fat 8.5g Protein 7.2g Carbs 0.2g
Ingredients:
- 1/2 cup of cheddar cheese shredded
- 1 teaspoon of salt
- 1/4 cup of heavy cream
- 12 eggs large
- 1 teaspoon of pepper

Instructions:
- Preheat your air fryer at 3570°F. Using the baking paper, grease a rimmed sheet pan using cooking spray.
- Crack the eggs into a medium-sized mixing bowl. In a mixing bowl, combine the shredded cheese, heavy cream, pepper, and salt.
- Spread the egg mixture equally over the prepared baking sheet and place it in an air fryer basket.
- Cook for around 10-15 minutes or till the eggs are cooked and no longer jiggly.
- Using a pizza cutter or knife, cut the pizza into 12-15 slices.

29. Air Fried Buffalo Breakfast Egg Cups

Preparation time: 10 minutes
Cooking time: 20 minutes
Servings: 4
Nutrition facts (Per serving) Calories 354 Total fat 22.3g Protein 21.0g Carbs 2.3g
Ingredients:
- 1/2 cup of cooked and chopped chicken
- 2 tablespoons of buffalo sauce
- 1/2 cup of sharp Cheddar cheese shredded
- 4 eggs large
- 2 oz. of cream cheese

Instructions:
- Break the eggs into four ramekins, one at a time.
- Combine buffalo sauce, cream cheese, and cheddar in a microwave-safe bowl. Microwave for about 20 seconds, stirring halfway through. Place a dollop of the melted mixture on top of the eggs in each ramekin and top with the chicken.
- Place the ramekins in an air fryer basket and cook for around 15 minutes at 320°F.

30. Air Fried Breakfast Farmer's Casserole

Preparation time: 10 minutes
Cooking time: 30 minutes
Servings: 6

Nutrition facts (Per serving) Calories 252 Total Fat 14g Protein 17g Carbs 14g

Ingredients:
- 1/4 cup of chopped green onions
- 1 can (12 ounces) of evaporated milk
- 3/4 cup of shredded Monterey jack cheese
- 1/2 teaspoon of salt
- 3 cups of shredded frozen hash brown potatoes
- 1 cup of cubed fully cooked ham
- 4 eggs large
- 1/4 teaspoon of pepper

Instructions:
- Fill an 8-inch baking dish halfway with potatoes and top with ham, onions, and cheese. Whisk together the salt, milk, eggs, and pepper inside a medium-sized mixing dish. Cover and refrigerate the egg mixture over the potatoes for several hours or overnight.
- Remove the dish from the refrigerator 30 minutes before cooking and discard the cover.
- Transfer the dish to the air fryer basket and cook for around 18 to 20 minutes at 375°F in the preheated air fryer.

Chapter 3: Appetizer and Snack Recipes

1. Air Fried Parmesan Garlic Oil-Free Chips

Preparation time: 10 minutes
Cooking time: 55 minutes
Servings: 1
Nutrition facts (Per serving) Calories 37 Total Fat 1g Protein 1g Carbs 5g
Ingredients:
- 2 Large Red Potatoes
- 4 cloves of garlic crushed
- 2 teaspoons of salt
- 2 tablespoons of homemade parmesan vegan

Instructions:
- Cut the potatoes into thin slices.
- Half-fill a bowl with water and add the cut potatoes. To the mixture, add 2 teaspoons of salt. Allow for 30 minutes of soak time.
- Drain and rinse potato slices. Allow to dry. Mix in the garlic powder and vegan parmesan cheese.
- Place half of the potato slices in the air fryer. If the air fryer is overcrowded, the chips will not cook evenly.
- Air fry potatoes for around 20-25 minutes at 170°F or till dry to the touch and no longer flimsy. Toss and stir the basket every 5 minutes or so.
- Raise the temperature at 400°F and cook for another 5 minutes, or till the potatoes are crispy.
- Remove from the air fryer and top with vegan parmesan cheese or salt. Repeat with the rest of the potato slices.

2. Air Fried Cheddar-Sausage Bites

Preparation time: 10 minutes
Cooking time: 25 minutes
Servings: 50-55 bites
Nutrition facts (Per serving) Calories 63 Fat 4g Protein 2g Carbs 2g
Ingredients:
- 1/2 large grated onion
- 1/4 teaspoon of black pepper
- 8 ounces of cheddar cheese shredded
- 1 1/4 cups of almond or coconut flour
- 16 ounces of breakfast sausage bulk
- 1 1/2 teaspoons of baking powder
- 1/2 teaspoon of cayenne pepper
- 3 tablespoons of melted unsalted butter
- 1/2 teaspoon of kosher salt

Instructions:
- Preheat your air fryer at 390°F and coat the air fryer basket using cooking spray.

- Inside a large-sized mixing bowl, combine the flour, baking powder, salt, cayenne pepper, and black pepper. To coat the shredded cheese evenly, toss it in the flour mixture. Mix in the onion, sausage, and melted butter till everything is combined. Using your hands, create 1-inch balls out of the mixture. Place the meatballs in a greased air fryer basket and spray using cooking spray.
- Cook for approximately 15-20 minutes. Enjoy when still warm!

3. Air Fried Stuffed Cherry Peppers

Preparation time: 10 minutes
Cooking time: 20 minutes
Servings: 25 peppers
Nutrition facts (Per serving) Calories 46 Fat 3.5g Protein 1.9g Carbs 1.2g
Ingredients:
- 1/4 pound of sausage
- 1 (14 ounces) jar of cherry peppers
- 1/4 cup of Parmesan cheese grated
- 1 egg
- 1/4 pound of ground beef

Instructions:
- Preheat your air fryer at 390°F. After removing all of the seeds from the peppers, drain them.
- Inside a large-sized mixing bowl, combine the bacon, ground beef, egg, and cheese. Fill peppers with the meat mixture after fully mixing.
- In a preheated air fryer, air fry for around 10-15 minutes. Allow for a few minutes of cooling before serving.

4. Air Fried Stuffed Mini Sweet Peppers

Preparation time: 10 minutes
Cooking time: 15 minutes
Servings: 16
Nutrition facts (Per serving) Calories 176 Total Fat 13.4g Protein 7.4g Carbs 2.7g
Ingredients:
- 8 mini sweet peppers
- 4 of crumbled and cooked slices of bacon
- 1/4 cup of cheddar cheese shredded
- 4 oz. of softened cream cheese

Instructions:
- Remove the pepper tops and cut each pepper lengthwise in half. Using a little knife, remove the seeds and membranes.
- Inside a small-sized mixing bowl, combine the bacon, cream cheese, and cheddar cheese.
- Load 3 teaspoons of the mixture into each sweet pepper and smooth it out. Place it in the frying basket.
- Preheat the air fryer at 400°F and set the timer for 8 minutes.

5. Bacon Wrapped Brussels Sprouts

Preparation time: 10 minutes
Cooking time: 30 minutes
Servings: 8
Nutrition facts (Per serving) Calories 267 Total Fat 24.3g Protein 6.5g Carbs 6.6g
Ingredients:
- 24 medium Brussels sprouts (1 pound 1-inch sprouts; cut any big ones in half)
- 1/4 cup of sugar-free maple syrup
- 12 strips of bacon (cut them in half to make shorter pieces)
- 1/8 teaspoon of cayenne pepper

For the dipping sauce:
- 1/2 teaspoon of garlic powder
- 1/2 tablespoon of Dijon mustard
- 1 tablespoon of sugar-free maple syrup
- 1/2 cup of mayonnaise
- 1/8 teaspoon of cayenne pepper

Instructions:
- Heat the air fryer at 390°F. Line a baking sheet using parchment paper.
- Arrange the short (halved) bacon bits on the baking sheet in a single layer. Brush them with maple syrup and season with cayenne pepper.
- Flip the bacon bits over to ensure the maple syrup is on the bottom. Roll up each

bacon slice with a Brussels sprout at the end. Place the baking sheet seam-side down. Repeat the process with the remaining sprouts. Brush the Brussels sprouts and bacon with the remaining maple syrup.
- Place the baking sheet in the air fryer basket and cook for around 15-20 minutes.
- In the meantime, make the dipping sauce inside a small-sized bowl. Inside a mixing bowl, whisk together the mayonnaise, maple syrup, mustard, cayenne pepper, and garlic powder till smooth.
- Serve immediately with prepared dipping sauce.

6. Air Fried Crispy Salmon Jerky

Preparation time: 10 minutes
Cooking time: 4 hours 5 minutes
Servings: 4
Nutrition facts (Per serving) Calories 108 Total Fat 4.1g Protein 15.1g Carbs 0.8g
Ingredients:
- 4 dashes of hot sauce
- 2 teaspoons liquid smoke flavoring
- 1/4 cup of soy sauce
- 1 tablespoon of lemon juice
- 2 tablespoons of Worcestershire sauce
- 1 lb. of skin removed salmon fillet
- 1/2 teaspoon of ground ginger
- 1 tablespoon of lemon juice

Instructions:
- Cut the fish into 4" long, 1/4" thick slices.
- Inside a big storage bag or a sealed tub, combine the remaining ingredients and apply them to the strips. Allow to marinate in the refrigerator for about 2 hours.
- Place each strip in the air fryer basket in a single layer.
- Set the air fryer temperature to 140°F and the timer for 4 hours.

7. Air Fried Seasoned Apple Chips

Preparation time: 10 minutes
Cooking time: 30 minutes
Servings: 2
Nutrition facts (Per serving) Calories 36 Total Fat 0.1g Protein 0.2g Carbs 9.5g
Ingredients:
- 1 cored apple
- 1/2 tablespoon of chili-lime seasoning or more to taste

Instructions:
- Start by preheating your air fryer at 180°F.
- Thinly slice the apple using a mandolin slicer.
- Fill the air fryer basket with as many apple slices as you can without them touching.
- Cook for around 12 minutes in an air fryer, in batches, if necessary. Remove the basket, flip the apple slices, and cook for another 8 to 12 minutes or till the other side is gently browned. Immediately season using chili-lime seasoning.

8. Air Fried Baba Ghanoush (Lebanese Appetizer)

Preparation time: 10 minutes
Cooking time: 35 minutes
Servings: 6
Nutrition facts (Per serving) Calories 215 Total Fat 18.6g Protein 3.7g Carbs 11.1g
Ingredients:
- 2 tablespoons of lemon juice
- 1/4 teaspoon of ground cumin
- 1 medium halved lengthwise eggplant
- 5 1/2 tablespoons of extra virgin olive oil, divided
- 1/2 teaspoon of lemon zest
- 1/8 teaspoon of smoked paprika
- 1 tablespoon of fresh parsley chopped
- 1/4 cup of tahini (paste of sesame seed)
- 1 bulb of garlic
- 2 tablespoons of feta cheese crumbled
- 1/2 teaspoon of kosher salt

Instructions:
- Preheat the air fryer at 400°F.

- Season the cut sides of the eggplant using salt. Allow for 20 to 30 minutes of rest. Blot dry using paper towels.
- Brush the cut sides of the eggplant with 1 tablespoon of olive oil. Remove 1/4 inch of the garlic bulb's top to expose the cloves. After coating the cloves with 1/2 tablespoon olive oil, wrap the bulb in aluminum foil. Place the eggplant and garlic in the air fryer basket.
- Cook in a preheated air fryer for 15 to 20 minutes or till the eggplant and garlic are soft, and the eggplant is a rich golden brown color. Remove from the air fryer and lay aside for 10 minutes to cool.
- Scoop the eggplant flesh into a food processor tub. Using a food processor, blend in the tahini, lemon juice, 4 roasted garlic cloves (save remaining roasted garlic for later use), remaining 4 tablespoons of olive oil, paprika, and cumin till smooth. Top with feta cheese, parsley, and lemon zest.

9. Air Fried Cheesy Popcorn

Preparation time: 10 minutes
Cooking time: 10 minutes
Servings: 4
Nutrition facts (Per serving) Calories 128 Total Fat 10.1g Protein 8g Carbs 1.2g
Ingredients:
- 1 1/2 tablespoons of cheddar cheese powder
- 3/4 teaspoon of sweet corn extract
- 1/2 tablespoon of butter flavored coconut oil
- 4 oz. of Provolone cheese (slice them into 1/2-inch cubes)

Instructions:
- Heat the air fryer at 390°F. Line a baking sheet using parchment paper.
- Place the 1/2-inch cheese slices on the parchment paper, leaving at least an inch between them. Cook for 2-4 minutes in the air fryer or until the cheese slices melt slightly and create rounder edges.
- Take the baking sheet out of the air fryer. If the cheese spreads too much, use a tiny spatula or your fingertips to gently press the edges inward while it's still soft. The chunks should be round and thicker than regular sliced cheese. Allow them to cool completely.
- Just before serving, stir together the butter-flavored coconut oil and corn extract inside a small-sized bowl.
- Mix the popcorn with the melted butter. Stir in the cheddar cheese powder and toss again.

10. Air Fried Cheesy Cauliflower Bread Sticks

Preparation time: 10 minutes
Cooking time: 35 minutes
Servings: 6
Nutrition facts (Per serving) Calories 214 Total Fat 14g Protein 15g Carbs 7g
Ingredients:
- 3/4 teaspoon of sea salt
- 1 cup of shredded Mozzarella cheese
- 2 cloves of minced garlic
- 1 tablespoon of melted butter
- 1/4 teaspoon of black pepper
- 1 head of cauliflower (rice using food processor or grater)
- 1/2 cup of hemp seeds
- Fresh parsley for garnishing
- 2 eggs large

Instructions:
- Place riced cauliflower inside a microwave-safe dish. Microwave for 10 minutes on high or till softened (or steam on the stove). Cool for a while.
- Preheat your air fryer at 390 degrees Fahrenheit. Line a baking sheet using parchment paper.
- While the cauliflower cools, pulse the hemp seeds in a blender or food processor till smooth.
- Inside a mixing bowl, combine the eggs, garlic, sea salt, and black pepper. Rep till the mixture is completely smooth.
- Place the cauliflower in a tea towel and squeeze it several times to extract as much juice as possible. You should be able to extract around one cup of fluid.

- Fill half of the food processor using drained riced cauliflower. Blend till completely smooth.
- Place the "dough" on the prepared baking sheet. Form into a 1/3-inch thick rectangle. Place the baking sheet in the air fryer basket.
- In a preheated air fryer, cook for around 10 to 15 minutes.
- Melted butter should be brushed on top. Cover with shredded mozzarella and cook for 5-10 minutes longer or till the cheese melts.
- Allow it to cool somewhat before cutting it into 24 breadstick-shaped rectangles by cutting lengthwise in half, then crosswise into 1-inch wide strips.

11. Crispy Bacon Wrapped Asparagus

Preparation time: 10 minutes
Cooking time: 20 minutes
Servings: 6
Nutrition facts (Per serving) Calories 202 Total Fat 18g Protein 66g Carbs 3g
Ingredients:
- 24 stalks of trimmed asparagus
- Garlic salt to taste
- 1 teaspoon of olive oil
- 12 slices of bacon (center cut)
- Black pepper to taste

Instructions:
- Start by preheating your air fryer at 400°F.
- Remove the woody ends of the asparagus. Drizzle using extra virgin olive oil to finish. Add garlic, salt, and black pepper to taste. (A small bit of oil is required to adhere to the salt and pepper.)
- Cut the bacon pieces lengthwise to produce shorter strips. Wrap each bacon strip tightly around each asparagus stem, slightly overlapping the bacon on each stalk. Arrange on the air fry basket, ensure they don't overlap and cook in batches as necessary.
- Cook for around 10 to 15 minutes in the air fryer; after 5 minutes, flip the asparagus and cook for another 5 minutes.

12. Air Fried Parmesan Cheddar Crisps

Preparation time: 10 minutes
Cooking time: 15 minutes
Servings: 4
Nutrition facts (Per serving) Calories 152 Total Fat 11g Protein 11g Carbs 1g
Ingredients:
- 3/4 cup of cheddar cheese shredded
- 1 teaspoon of Italian seasoning
- 3/4 cup of parmesan cheese shredded

Instructions:
- Start by preheating your air fryer at 400°F. Line a baking sheet using parchment paper.
- Combine the cheeses inside a small-sized mixing bowl.
- On a baking sheet, space heaping scoops of shredded cheese 2 inches (5 cm) apart. (Make sure to provide enough area for them to spread.) Season to taste with Italian seasoning.
- Place the sheet in the air fryer basket and cook in batches. Cook for about 5 minutes in a hot air fryer or till the chips begin to color and crisp.
- Allow the cheese chips to cool slightly before placing them on a platter.

13. Air Fried Kale Chips

Preparation time: 10 minutes
Cooking time: 16 minutes
Servings: 1
Nutrition facts (Per serving) Calories 159 Total Fat 8g Protein 7g Carbs 20g

Ingredients:
- 1 teaspoon of sesame seeds (black or white)

- 6 cups of torn Lacinato kale leaves packed (remove the stems and ribs)
- 1 tablespoon of olive oil
- 1/4 teaspoon of poppy seeds
- 1/2 teaspoon of dried minced garlic
- 1 teaspoon of soy sauce lower-sodium

Instructions:

- Before breaking the kale leaves into 1 1/2-inch pieces, wash and dry them. Inside a medium-sized mixing bowl, combine the kale, olive oil, and soy sauce, gently massaging the leaves to coat.
- Cook for around 6 to 10 minutes at 375°F with 1/3 of the kale leaves in the air fryer basket, shaking halfway through. While the kale chips are still wet, sprinkle sesame seeds, garlic, and poppy seeds equally over them.

14. Air Fried Asparagus Tots

Preparation time: 10 minutes
Cooking time: 20 minutes
Servings: 2 (10 tots)
Nutrition facts (Per serving) Calories 78 Total Fat 3.2g Protein 7.5g Carbs 6.9g
Ingredients:

- 1/4 cup of grated Parmesan cheese
- Cooking spray
- 12 ounces of trimmed and diced asparagus
- 1/2 cup of panko bread crumbs

Instructions:

- Bring salted water to a boil over a medium-high flame. Boil the asparagus for around 5 minutes. Drain in a colander and let aside for 5 minutes to cool or till readily treated.
- Combine the asparagus, parmesan cheese, and breadcrumbs inside a large-sized mixing dish. Knead everything together with your hands till it resembles dough. To make a tot, roll 1 tablespoon of the ingredients into a ball. Place on a serving platter. Repeat with the remaining mixture. Freeze the tater tots for 30 minutes.
- Preheat the air fryer at 400°F.
- Spray the air fryer basket liberally using nonstick cooking oil. Cooking spray the outside of the tots before placing them in the basket. Cook for around 10 minutes, shaking the pan halfway through to ensure even cooking.

15. Air Fried Cheesy Crackers

Preparation time: 10 minutes
Cooking time: 25 minutes
Servings: 8
Nutrition facts (Per serving) Calories 174 Total Fat 14g Protein 8g Carbs 5g
Ingredients:

- 1 tablespoon of nutritional yeast (optional)
- 1/4 teaspoon of sea salt
- 3/4 cup of cheddar cheese shredded
- 1 1/2 cups of almond flour blanched
- 1 egg large

Instructions:

- Melt the cheddar cheese in the microwave till it becomes creamy and easy to stir. Inside a medium-sized mixing bowl, combine the almond flour, nutritional yeast, and sea salt. Stir in the egg till fully combined. The mixture will be crumbly.
- Mix in the melted cheese and knead everything together using your hands.
- Form the dough into a large ball. If it's too sticky to handle, chill it for about 15 minutes.
- Place the dough ball between two sheets of parchment paper that have been lightly oiled. Roll to a very small rectangle with a thickness of 1/16 inch (.2 cm) to 1/8 inch (.4 cm).
- Preheat the air fryer at 400°F. Line a baking sheet using parchment paper.
- Place the crackers in squares or rectangles on the lined baking sheet. Prick the holes using a fork or toothpick to halt the bubbling.
- Transfer the baking sheet to the air fryer basket and cook for about 15 minutes or till the top and edges are lightly golden. Allow to cool to crisp the crackers.

16. Air Fried Deviled Eggs

Preparation time: 10 minutes

Cooking time: 30 minutes
Servings: 12 halves of deviled eggs
Nutrition facts (Per serving) Calories 63 Total Fat 5.3g Protein 3.3g Carbs 0.8g
Ingredients:
- 1 thinly sliced green onion
- 1 teaspoon of Dijon mustard
- 1 1/2 teaspoons of sesame oil
- 6 eggs large
- 1 1/2 teaspoons of sriracha sauce
- Sesame seeds toasted
- 1 teaspoon of ginger root finely grated
- 2 tablespoons of mayonnaise
- 1 teaspoon of soy sauce low-sodium
- 1 teaspoon of rice vinegar

Instructions:
- Place the eggs in an air fryer basket, leaving enough room between them for air circulation. Set the timer for 15 minutes and preheat the air fryer at 260°F. Close the air fryer's lid.
- Remove the eggs from the air fryer and place them in a bowl of ice water for 10 minutes to cool. Take the eggs out of the water and peel and cut them in half.
- Scoop out the yolks and place them in a tiny food processor. Inside a large-sized mixing bowl, combine mayonnaise, sesame oil, sriracha, low-sodium soy sauce, ginger root, Dijon mustard, and rice vinegar. Process till everything is well combined, and the mixture is smooth and mousse-like.
- Fill a piping bag halfway with the yolk mixture and pipe a heaping spoonful through the egg white; you may also do this with a spoon. As a garnish, sprinkle with sesame seeds and green onion.

17. Air Fried Falafel

Preparation time: 10 minutes
Cooking time: 30 minutes
Servings: 15 falafels
Nutrition facts (Per serving) Calories 60 Total Fat 1.1g Protein 3.1g Carbs 9.9g
Ingredients:
- 2 tablespoons of chickpea flour
- 1 clove of garlic
- 1 1/2 cups of stems removed fresh cilantro
- 1 cup of dry garbanzo beans
- 3/4 cup of stems removed fresh flat-leafed parsley
- 1 red onion small
- 1 tablespoon of sriracha sauce
- 1/2 teaspoon of baking powder
- Cooking spray
- 1/4 teaspoon of baking soda
- 1 tablespoon of ground cumin
- Black pepper and salt to taste
- 1 tablespoon of ground coriander

Instructions:
- Soak the chickpeas in a large amount of water for 24 hours. Rub the chickpea skins with your fingertips to loosen and remove them. Thoroughly rinse and drain. Spread the chickpeas out on a large clean cloth to dry.
- Mix cilantro, parsley, chickpeas, garlic, and onion in a food processor till a rough mixture forms. Pour the contents into a large-sized mixing bowl. Combine the chickpea flour, cumin, coriander, salt, sriracha, and pepper. After covering the bowl, let it rest for about an hour.
- Start by preheating your air fryer at 375°F.
- Mix in the baking soda and baking powder with the chickpea mixture. Mix using your hands till everything is well combined. Form 15 equal-sized balls into patties by gently pressing them together. Coat falafel patties in cooking mist.
- In a preheated air fryer, cook falafel patties for around 10 to 15 minutes. Cook the rest of the falafel in batches.

18. Air Fried Pizza Muffins

Preparation time: 10 minutes
Cooking time: 30 minutes
Servings: 10
Nutrition facts (Per serving) Calories 117 Total Fat 8g Protein 8g Carbs 4g
Ingredients:
- 1/2 teaspoon of black pepper
- 1 1/4 cups of shredded mozzarella

- 2 eggs large
- 1 tablespoon of melted butter
- 2 shredded medium zucchini
- 1/2 teaspoon of salt
- 2 tablespoons of coconut flour

For the topping:
- 1 oz. of pepperoni slices
- 1/4 cup of marinara sauce
- 2/3 cup of mozzarella shredded
- 1 teaspoon of Italian seasoning

Instructions:
- Preheat your air fryer for 3 minutes at 390°F and grease a muffin tray using cooking spray.
- Combine all of the ingredients indicated above inside a large-sized mixing bowl. Cut a piece of parchment paper to fit your air fryer basket.
- Inside a large-sized mixing bowl, combine the shredded zucchini, coconut flour, shredded mozzarella, black pepper, and sea salt. Incorporate the melted butter and eggs.
- Fill the muffin cups evenly with the zucchini mixture, packing it down the sides and smoothing the tops. Place the muffin pan within the air fryer basket.
- Cook for around 15-20 minutes or till firm and golden on top.
- Place a spoonful of marinara sauce and the remaining mozzarella cheese on top of each zucchini bite. Season with Italian spice and pepperoni pieces to taste.

19. Air Fried Garlic-Almond Crackers

Preparation time: 10 minutes
Cooking time: 20 minutes
Servings: 12
Nutrition facts (Per serving) Calories 72 Fat 5.7g Protein 3.1g, Carbs 3.1g
Ingredients:
- 1/2 cup of almond meal
- 1/3 cup of Parmesan cheese shredded
- 1/2 teaspoon of salt
- 1 teaspoon of garlic powder
- 1/2 cup of ground flax seed
- 1/2 cup of water

Instructions:
- Preheat your air fryer at 400°F. Line a baking sheet using parchment paper.
- Combine ground flaxseed, almond meal, water, Parmesan cheese, garlic powder, and salt inside a medium-sized mixing dish. Allow 3 to 5 minutes for the water to settle and the dough to bind.
- Place the dough on the prepared baking sheet, covered with waxed paper or plastic wrap. Flatten the dough to 1/8-inch thickness with a rolling pin or your fingertips. Take off the waxed paper. Make indentations in the dough with a knife to indicate where the crackers will be broken apart.
- Cook the sheet in the air fryer for around 15 minutes or till golden brown.

20. Air Fried Bacon Wrapped Scallops

Preparation time: 10 minutes
Cooking time: 15 minutes
Servings: 4
Nutrition facts (Per serving) Calories 196 Fat 16g Protein 10g Carbs 2g
Ingredients:
- 1/2 teaspoon of lemon pepper
- 1 clove of minced garlic
- 12 of large sea scallops
- 6 slices of bacon
- 1 teaspoon of parsley
- Salt and pepper to season
- 1 tablespoon of melted butter

Instructions:
- Preheat your air fryer at 390°F.
- Cook bacon inside a medium-sized frying pan for 4 to 5 minutes on each side. (Prevent crisping)
- Season the scallops using salt and pepper after drying them with paper towels.
- Wrap the scallops in bacon and stack three on each wooden skewer.

- Brush the tops of the scallops with the melted butter, parsley, garlic, and lemon pepper.
- Coat the air fryer basket using cooking oil. Place the bacon-wrapped scallops in the basket in a single layer; if necessary, divide them into two groups.
- Cook for around 8 to 10 minutes in the air fryer.

21. Air Fried Sausage Stuffed Mushrooms

Preparation time: 10 minutes
Cooking time: 20 minutes
Servings: 24 mushrooms
Nutrition facts (Per serving) Calories 64 Fat 5g Protein 3g Carbs 1g
Ingredients:
- 24 mushrooms
- 2 ounces of cheddar cheese
- 1/4 cup of parmesan cheese shredded
- 4 ounces of cream cheese
- 2 cloves garlic
- 1/2 pound of sausage(optional)
- 2 tablespoons of onion minced

Instructions:
- Preheat your air fryer at 390°F.
- Remove the stems from the mushrooms to clean them. Scoop off the center of the mushrooms to make a hole for filling.
- Inside a small-sized skillet, finely dice the stems and combine them with the sausage, onion, and garlic. Cook till the sauce's color changes. Remove the fat.
- Set aside 1/4 cup of the parmesan and cheddar cheese mixture for topping.
- Combine the cheese, cream cheese, and sausage inside a small-sized mixing bowl. Fill up the holes in each mushroom with the filling.
- Top with the reserved 1/4 cup of cheese and cook for 10 to 15 minutes or till the cheese melts.

22. Air-Fried Zucchini Bites

Preparation time: 10 minutes
Cooking time: 30 minutes
Servings: 24 to 36 bites
Nutrition facts (Per serving) Calories 51.3 Fat 3.2 g Protein 2.3 g Carbs 3.6 g
Ingredients:
- 1 tablespoon of olive oil
- 1/4 cup of cream
- 3 eggs
- 1 large zucchini grated
- 1 large carrot grated
- 3 slices of finely sliced bacon
- 1 cup of grated cheese
- 1/2 cup of self-rising flour
- 1 onion chopped

Instructions:
- Heat the oil in a big skillet and sauté the onion till it is transparent. Simmer till the bacon turns color, then add the zucchini and carrots and cook for around 2 to 3 minutes more. Allow it to cool for a few minutes.
- In a separate medium-sized mixing bowl, combine the milk, eggs, and cheese; add the egg mixture to the zucchini mixture and stir in the flour.
- Fill halfway with the zucchini bits' mixture in each floured and greased muffin cup.
- Air fry for around 15 to 20 minutes at 350°F or till done.

23. Cheesy Pizza Pepperoni Puffs

Preparation time: 10 minutes
Cooking time: 30 minutes
Servings: 10 puffs
Nutrition facts (Per serving) Calories 160 Fat 9g Protein 9g Carbs 10g
Ingredients:
- 3/4 cup of mini pepperoni
- 1 egg lightly beaten
- 3/4 cup of Almond flour
- 1/2 diced red or green pepper
- 3/4 cup of low-fat milk
- 4 strings of mozzarella cheese
- 1/2 cup of pizza sauce readymade

- 3/4 teaspoon of oregano
- 1 cup of shredded cheese (cheddar or mozzarella)
- 1/2 teaspoon of garlic powder
- 1/2 teaspoon of basil
- 1 teaspoon of baking powder

Instructions:
- Preheat your air fryer at 370°F. Grease a muffin tray using cooking oil. Combine the flour, spices, and baking powder inside a mixing dish. Mix in the milk and egg till completely mixed.
- Set aside for 10 minutes after adding the shredded cheese, pepperoni, and red pepper.
- Fill each muffin cup halfway with the mixture. Divide each cheese string into three pieces and insert one into each muffin. Place the muffin pan in the air fryer basket.
- Air fry for around 15-20 minutes.

24. Air Fried Cheesy Olives

Preparation time: 10 minutes
Cooking time: 20 minutes
Servings: 9
Nutrition facts(Per serving)
Calories 110 Fat 8g Protein 4g Carbs 5.7g
Ingredients:
- 1 cup of Cheddar cheese shredded
- 1/2 cup of almond flour
- 24 green stuffed olives pimento
- 1/8 teaspoon of cayenne pepper
- 2 tablespoons of softened butter

Instructions:
- Preheat your air fryer at 350°F.
- Inside a medium-sized mixing bowl, combine the butter and cheese, then whisk in the cayenne pepper and flour. Thoroughly combine. Wrap a tablespoon of dough around each green olive and roll it into a ball in your palms. Arrange the olives on a baking sheet coated using parchment paper. Place the sheet of parchment paper in the air fryer basket.
- In a preheated air fryer, cook for 15 minutes or till light golden brown.

25. Air Fried Brie and Artichoke

Preparation time: 10 minutes
Cooking time: 20 minutes
Servings: 12
Nutrition facts (Per serving) Calories 200 Fat 16.3g Protein 12.2g Carbs 1.5g
Ingredients:
- 2 cloves of minced garlic
- 6 slices of minced sun-dried tomatoes in oil
- 1 Brie cheese round (1 1/2 pounds)
- 3 chopped and drained artichoke hearts packed in oil

Instructions:
- Preheat your air fryer at 350°F.
- Combine the garlic artichoke hearts, sundried tomatoes, and olive oil inside a medium-sized cup.
- Brie cheese's top rind should be trimmed and discarded.
- In a round baking dish, place the brie. Layer the tomato mixture on top.
- Cook for around 15 minutes in a hot air fryer till the cheese softens.

26. Apple Fritters with Cinnamon Sprinkle Topping

Preparation time: 10 minutes
Cooking time: 15 minutes
Servings: 12 fritters
Nutrition facts (Per serving) Calories 115 Fat 11g Protein 5g Carbs 2g
Ingredients:
- 2 tablespoons of Vanilla protein powder sugar-free
- 1/4 cup of granulated sugar substitute
- 1/2 cup apples finely chopped (approx. 1/4 inch pieces)
- 2/3 cup of almond milk unsweetened
- 1/4 teaspoon of ground nutmeg
- 1 tablespoon of melted butter
- 1/2 cup of coconut flour
- 2 teaspoons of baking powder
- 1 teaspoon of ground cinnamon

- 1/4 teaspoon of kosher salt
- Cooking Spray
- 2 eggs
- 1/4 teaspoon of xanthan gum

For the cinnamon sprinkle topping:
- 2 tablespoons of melted butter
- 1/4 cup of granulated sugar substitute
- 1.5 teaspoon of ground cinnamon

Instructions:
- Preheat your air fryer to 370°F.
- Inside a medium-sized mixing dish, combine all of the dry ingredients. Whisk together the eggs, almond milk, and melted butter inside a small-sized cup. In a mixing dish, combine the wet and dry ingredients, then whisk in the apples. Allow it to sit for 2 minutes. Form 12 densely packed balls. Place the fritters on a baking pan and rotate them.
- Air fry for around 10 to 15 minutes in the air fryer or till lightly golden brown.
- To make the cinnamon sprinkle topping, combine the cinnamon and sweetener inside a small-sized cup. Brush the fritters with melted butter before rolling them in the cinnamon/sweetener mixture.

27. Air Fryer Loaded Faux-Tato Skins

Preparation time: 10 minutes
Cooking time: 30 minutes
Servings: 12 skins
Nutrition facts (Per serving) Calories 115 Fat 9g Protein 9g Carbs 2g

Ingredients:
- 1 egg
- 1/4 cup of sour cream
- 2 cups of cheesy cauliflower puree
- 4 chopped and cooked slices of bacon
- 1 cup of cheddar cheese shredded
- 2 tablespoons of scallions chopped

Instructions:
- Well combine the egg and the cauliflower puree.
- Fill each muffin cup with 2 tablespoons of the mashed mixture. Spread the puree out to about a half-inch thickness on top and bottom. If it's too thin, it won't come out of the tin. Place the muffin cups in the air fryer basket. Cook them in batches if necessary.
- Air fry for about 20 minutes at 380°F or till dry and firm. Return them to the air fryer for a few minutes if they're still too soft.
- Place them on a greased baking sheet after carefully extracting them from the muffin cups with a butter knife.
- Fill them with cheese and bacon, then place them back in the air fryer for 5 minutes or until the cheese melts.
- When serving, sprinkle with sour cream and scallions or fresh herbs.

28. Air Fried Tasty Pickles

Preparation time: 10 minutes
Cooking time: 30 minutes
Servings: 4
Nutrition facts (Per serving) Calories 209 Total Fat 17g Protein 14g Carbs 1g

Ingredients:
- 32 medium drained dill rounds pickle
- 1/4 cup of isolate whey protein
- 3 tablespoons of avocado oil
- 1 large beaten egg
- 1/2 cup of parmesan cheese grated

Instructions:
- On paper towels, drain and dry the pickles.
- Whisk together the egg inside a small-sized dish large enough to hold 5 pickles.
- Inside a medium-sized mixing bowl, combine the protein powder and cheese till well combined.
- Coat 5-6 pickles completely in the egg wash. Shake off any excess egg before coating with the coating mixture. A fork makes it easy to flip the pickles. Preheat the air fryer at 400 degrees Fahrenheit. Brush the pickle tops and the air fryer basket using cooking oil. If necessary, air fry in batches to avoid any contact.

- Air fry for about 12 minutes; after that, flip the pickles and brush them with avocado oil again. Cook for another 4 to 5 minutes.

29. Air Fried Mozzarella Cheese Balls

Preparation time: 10 minutes
Cooking time: 30 minutes
Servings: 12
Nutrition facts (Per serving) Calories 206 Total Fat 14.6g Protein 13.3g Carbs 5.2g
Ingredients:
- 2 cups of shredded mozzarella
- 1 cup of seasoned Italian breadcrumbs
- 1 1/2 teaspoons of garlic powder
- 3 tablespoons of cornstarch
- 1 tablespoon of Italian seasoning
- 2 beaten eggs
- 1 1/2 teaspoons of Parmesan
- 3 tablespoons of water
- 1 teaspoon of sea salt

Instructions:
- Combine the mozzarella, Parmesan, cornstarch, and water inside a large mixing dish. Thoroughly combine.
- Roll the mixture into 1-inch bite-size balls and place on a baking sheet lined using parchment paper. Place for 1 hour in the freezer.
- Inside a small-sized cup, whisk together the eggs. Inside a separate dish, combine the breadcrumbs, Italian seasoning, garlic powder, and salt.
- Dip the cheeseballs in the eggs to coat them. After rolling in the breadcrumb mixture, return to the baking sheet. Return to the freezer for 20 minutes more.
- Remove the cheese balls from the freezer and coat them in the egg mixture again before rolling them in the breadcrumbs.
- Preheat the air fryer at 360 degrees Fahrenheit. Once the air fryer basket has warmed, place the cheese balls inside.
- Shake the air fryer every couple of minutes to ensure equal browning. When serving, serve with pizza or marinara sauce on the side.

30. Air Fried Cheesy Bacon Jalapeno Bread

Preparation time: 10 minutes
Cooking time: 25 minutes
Servings: 8
Nutrition facts (Per serving) Calories 273 Total Fat 18.1g Protein 20.1g Carbs 2.1g
Ingredients:
- 4 chopped and cooked bacon slices
- 1/4 cup of pickled jalapeños chopped
- 2 cups of cheddar cheese shredded
- 1/4 cup of Parmesan cheese grated
- 2 eggs large

Instructions:
- Combine all of the ingredients indicated above inside a large-sized mixing bowl. Cut a piece of parchment paper to fit your air fryer basket.
- Dampen your hands using a little spray and press the mixture into a circle. Depending on the size of your fryer, you may need to divide this into two smaller cheese bread slices.
- Place the parchment and cheese bread in the air fryer basket.
- Preheat the oven at 320°F and set a 15-minute timer.
- When there are 5 minutes left in the cooking time, gently flip the bread. When the bread is entirely cooked, the top will be golden brown. Enjoy when still warm!

Chapter 4: Lunch and Main Recipes

1. Air Fried Zucchini Skins with Buffalo Chicken

Preparation time: 10 minutes
Cooking time: 25 minutes
Servings: 8 pieces
Nutrition facts (Per serving) Calories 80 Fat 3g Protein 9.5g Carbs 3.5g
Ingredients:
- 2 zucchinis large, about 9 ounces each
- 1/4 teaspoon of paprika
- Olive oil spray
- 1/2 teaspoon of salt
- 1/4 teaspoon of garlic powder

For buffalo chicken stuffing
- 1/4 cup of light Blue Cheese or Ranch Dressing
- 2 tablespoons of scallions chopped
- 7 ounces of skinless chicken breasts shredded
- 1 ounce 1/3 less fat softened cream cheese
- 1/4 cup of hot sauce, and more for drizzling on top
- 4 teaspoons of blue cheese crumbled

Instructions:
- Cream together the cream cheese and spicy sauce in a medium-sized mixing bowl till smooth. Incorporate the chicken.
- Cut the zucchini in half lengthwise, then again to produce 8 slices. Scoop off all of the pulp from each piece, leaving a 1/4-inch shell (save pulp for another use).
- Spread the zucchini peels out on a work surface. Spray the cut side with olive oil, season with salt, then sprinkle with garlic powder and paprika.
- Cook for 8 minutes in batches at 350°F in the air fryer till tender-crisp. Fill each skin evenly with 3-4 tablespoons of buffalo chicken and 1/2 teaspoon of cheese. Cook for a further 2 minutes or till the cheese melts. Serve immediately with 1/2 tablespoon blue cheese dressing and scallions on top. Serve right away.

2. Air Fryer Cauliflower Steak Loaded

Preparation time: 10 minutes
Cooking time: 12 minutes
Servings: 2
Nutrition facts (Per serving) Calories 122 Fat 8.4g Protein 4.9g Carbs 4.7g
Ingredients:
- 12 oz. of cauliflower, slice into 2 steaks about 3/4-inch thick
- 1/4 cup of cheddar Ranch dressing for drizzling
- 2 tablespoons of extra virgin olive oil unfiltered
- 1/4 teaspoon of granulated garlic
- 1 pinch of cayenne pepper
- Kosher salt
- 1/4 cup of cheddar cheese shredded
- Freshly ground black pepper

Instructions:
- Inside a small-sized mixing dish, combine salt, cayenne pepper, pepper, garlic, and oil. Brush the mixture over the cauliflower.

- If necessary, work in batches. In the air fryer, place each cauliflower steak.
- Cook for 7 minutes in the air fryer at 400°F.
- Grate some shredded cheddar cheese over the steaks before serving. Drizzle the ranch dressing on top.

3. Air Fried Three Cheese Stuffed Zucchini Boats

Preparation time: 10 minutes
Cooking time: 35 minutes
Servings: 2
Nutrition facts (Per serving) Calories 215 Fat 14.9g Protein 10.5g Carbs 6.6g
Ingredients:
- 1/4 cup of tomato paste low carb
- 2 halved and cored medium zucchini
- 1/4 cup of blue cheese
- 1 tablespoon of olive oil
- 1/4 cup of Gouda cheese
- 2 tablespoons of Mozzarella cheese shredded
- 1/4 teaspoon of garlic powder
- 1/2 teaspoon of dried parsley
- 1/4 teaspoon of dried oregano

Instructions:
- Brush 2 tablespoons of spaghetti sauce into each zucchini shell.
- Inside a medium-sized mixing bowl, combine the Gouda, blue cheese, oregano, garlic powder, and parsley. Fill half of each zucchini shell with ingredients. Place the zucchini shells in the air fryer basket.
- Cook for about 20 minutes at 350°F. Serve immediately with a sprinkle of mozzarella cheese.

4. Air Fried Roasted Broccoli Salad

Preparation time: 10 minutes
Cooking time: 15 minutes
Servings: 2

Nutrition facts (Per serving) Calories 215 Fat 16.3g Protein 6.4g Carbs 7.1g
Ingredients:
- 3 cups of broccoli florets fresh
- 1/4 cup of almonds sliced
- 2 tablespoons of avocado oil
- 1/2 teaspoon of sea salt
- 1/4 cup of cranberries dried
- 1/2 lemon

Instructions:
- Half-fill a 6" round baking dish with broccoli. Drizzle the broccoli with oil. Combine the almonds and cranberries in a mixing bowl. Place the dish in the air fryer basket.
- Cook for about 7 minutes at 380°F.
- Sprinkle salt halfway through the cooking time.
- When finished, peel the lemon and squeeze the juice into the pan before serving.

5. Air Fried Cheesy Chicken Mushroom

Preparation time: 10 minutes
Cooking time: 30 minutes
Servings: 4
Nutrition facts (Per serving) Calories 311 Fat 16g Protein 33g Carbs 8g
Ingredients:
- 1/4 cup of sliced green onions
- 3 tablespoons of butter(divided)
- 1/2 cup of chicken broth
- 1/8 teaspoon of pepper
- 1/3 cup of Parmesan cheese grated
- 1 cup of sliced fresh mushrooms
- 1/4 cup of whole wheat flour
- 4 halves of chicken breast (1 pound) skinless and boneless
- 1/4 teaspoon of salt
- 1/3 cup of part-skim mozzarella cheese shredded

Instructions:

- Preheat your air fryer at 390°F. Flatten all chicken breast pieces to 1/4-inch thickness. Coat the chicken on both sides with flour in a medium-sized mixing dish.
- In 2 teaspoons of butter, brown the chicken on all sides. Grease a baking dish and place the chicken in it. Sauté the mushrooms in the remaining butter in the same pan till softened, then add the chicken broth, pepper, and salt. Cook for 5 minutes or till the liquid has been reduced to half a cup. Spread the sauce over the chicken inside a baking dish. Put the dish in the air fryer basket.
- Cook for approximately 15 minutes. After 10 minutes, sprinkle with green onions & cheese and bake for another 3 to 5 minutes.

6. Air Fried Peppers and Chicken

Preparation time: 10 minutes
Cooking time: 40 minutes
Servings: 6
Nutrition facts (Per serving) Calories 382 Fat 15g Protein 54g Carbs 6g
Ingredients:
- 10 chopped brown mushrooms or 2 Portobello mushrooms
- 1 medium finely chopped onion
- 1/2 teaspoon of salt
- 1 large grated garlic clove
- 2 chopped large bell peppers
- 1 tablespoon of coconut or avocado oil
- 3 tablespoons of chopped fresh parsley (optional)
- 1 cup shredded sharp cheese like cheddar, marble, Gouda, or Gruyere
- 3 lbs. of boneless and skinless chicken breasts or thighs
- Ground black pepper to taste

Instructions:
- Preheat your air fryer at 390°F. Cooking spray a baking dish large enough to hold your air fryer basket.
- Inside a large-sized baking dish, combine the chicken, salt, garlic, and pepper. To coat uniformly, combine all ingredients and distribute in a single layer. Place in the air fryer basket.
- Cook, covered, for about 15-20 minutes. The chicken is done when it is pale and surrounded by clear juices.
- Meanwhile, heat a large-sized ceramic nonstick skillet over low-medium flame, stirring it to coat it with oil. Cook, stirring occasionally, for a few minutes after adding the onion. Continue to sauté the mushrooms for a few minutes more, stirring occasionally. Cook for another 5 minutes after adding the bell peppers.
- Remove the chicken from the air fryer and set it aside. Separate the chicken into small pieces and top with vegetables (sprinkle on top) and cheese.
- Place the dish in the air fryer and cook for 5 minutes more. Serve immediately!

7. Air Fried Greek-Style Chicken Stir Fry

Preparation time: 10 minutes
Cooking time: 20 minutes
Servings: 2
Nutrition facts (Per serving) Calories 234 Fat 8.0g Protein 20.4g Carbs 3.9g
Ingredients:
- 1/2 coarsely chopped medium red onion
- 2 tablespoons of feta cheese crumbled
- 1/2 coarsely chopped red bell pepper
- 10 oz. of skinless, boneless chicken breast
- 1/2 coarsely chopped medium zucchini
- 1 teaspoon of dried oregano
- 1 1/2 tablespoons of avocado oil
- 1/2 teaspoon of dried thyme
- Salt and pepper
- 1/2 teaspoon of dried parsley
- 1/2 teaspoon of garlic powder

Instructions:
- Cut the chicken into 1-inch chunks.
- Combine the chicken, bell pepper, red onion, and zucchini inside a medium-sized mixing dish.

- Combine the parsley, oregano, garlic powder, and thyme in a mixing bowl. Season to taste with salt and pepper.
- Drizzle with oil and stir to coat everything evenly.
- Spread the mixture in the Air Fryer basket and cook at 380°F for 12 to 15 minutes. Halfway through the cooking time, shake the basket.
- Serve garnished with feta cheese.

8. Air Fried Turkey Burgers

Preparation time: 10 minutes
Cooking time: 25 minutes
Servings: 6
Nutrition facts (Per serving) Calories 92 Fat 2g Protein 18g Carbs 1g
Ingredients:
- 1 teaspoon of cumin
- 1/2 teaspoon of salt
- 1 lb. of lean ground turkey
- 1/4 teaspoon of ground black pepper
- 1 1/2 cups of zucchini about 1 medium, finely shredded
- 1 large grated garlic clove

Instructions:
- Inside a large-sized mixing bowl, combine zucchini, ground turkey, garlic, cumin, salt, and pepper. Use your hands to completely combine the ingredients.
- Make 6 large turkey burger patties out of the ground turkey, about the size of a medium hand. Flatten the burgers because they "leap up" when cooked. Wet hands can assist with the stickiness. Coat them with frying oil spray and place them in the air fryer basket.
- Cook for around 15 minutes at 370°F.
- Sandwich the patties with whole grain or thin multigrain bread. Serve "naked" with homemade guacamole and store-bought salsa.

9. Air Fried Roasted Whole Lemon Cauliflower

Preparation time: 10 minutes
Cooking time: 20 minutes
Servings: 4
Nutrition facts (Per serving) Calories 91 Fat 5.7g Protein 3g Carbs 4g
Ingredients:
- 2 tablespoons melted butter
- 1 teaspoon of Italian seasonings
- 2 tablespoons of olive oil
- Salt and pepper to taste
- 1 head of cauliflower, leaves removed
- 2 cloves of crushed garlic
- 1/2 lemon

Instructions:
- Brush the cauliflower head using melted butter. Inside a small-sized cup, combine the butter, salt, oil, pepper, spices, and crushed garlic.
- After properly coating the cauliflower head with seasoning mix, place it in the air fryer basket.
- Cook for about 15 minutes at 350°F. Squeeze half a lemon over the cauliflower before serving.

10. Air Fried Cheese Garlic Rolls

Preparation time: 10 minutes
Cooking time: 15 minutes
Servings: 4
Nutrition facts (Per serving) Calories 199 Fat 14.9g Protein 12.37g Carbs 3.18g
Ingredients:
- 1/2 cup of almond flour
- 3/4 cup of mozzarella cheese shredded
- Salt and ground black pepper
- 1/4 cup of parmesan cheese grated
- 1/2 teaspoon of garlic powder
- 1/4 teaspoon of Italian powder

Instructions:
- Place a piece of aluminum foil or parchment paper in the air-fryer basket and coat it using cooking spray.
- Bring a small to medium-sized pot halfway full of water to the boil.

- Inside a large-sized mixing bowl, combine the mozzarella cheese, almond flour, garlic powder, and salt. Form a smooth ball from each section.
- Inside a small-sized cup, combine the Italian powder, Parmesan cheese, pepper, and garlic powder. Before placing the rolls in the air fryer basket, coat them in the herb and cheese mixture.
- Cook for about 13 minutes at 400°F or till crispy and gently browned.

11. Air Fried Stir-Fry Broccoli and Beef

Preparation time: 10 minutes
Cooking time: 1 hour
Servings: 4
Nutrition facts (Per serving) Calories 430 Fat 12g Protein 15g Carbs 10g
Ingredients:
- 1 1/2 lbs. of Thinly Sliced Steak, 1-inch pieces
- 2 teaspoons of ginger paste
- 3 tablespoons of Granular Sweetener
- 2 tablespoons of Avocado oil, divided
- 1/4 teaspoon of crushed red pepper
- 1 tablespoon of Minced Garlic
- 1/2 cup of Soy Sauce (gluten-free)
- 4 cups of Broccoli Florets
- 1/2 teaspoon of sesame seeds
- 1/8 teaspoon of xanthan gum

Instructions:
- Inside a large-sized mixing dish or storage bag, add the meat, ginger, soy sauce, garlic, avocado oil, and granular sweetener to marinate. Allow 1 hour to marinate in the refrigerator.
- Reserving the marinade, remove the steak from the marinade and place it in the air fryer basket.
- Cook for around 20 minutes at 320°F. After 10 minutes, add broccoli and pepper to the air fryer basket and shake gently.
- Inside a skillet over medium flame, bring the marinade to the boil, then lower it to a low flame. Stir in the xanthan gum to allow it to thicken.
- In a skillet over medium flame, bring the marinade to the boil, then lower it to a low flame. Stir in the xanthan gum to allow it to thicken.
- When the air fryer's timer goes off, rapidly empty the fryer basket into the skillet and stir it with the marinade. On top, sprinkle some sesame seeds. Serve immediately.

12. Air Fried Spinach Gratin

Preparation time: 10 minutes
Cooking time: 30 minutes
Servings: 8
Nutrition facts (Per serving) Calories 170 Fat 13g Protein 9g Carbs 6g
Ingredients:
- 1 clove of minced garlic
- 20 ounces of chopped spinach frozen (two 10-ounce packages)
- 4 ounces of cream cheese
- 1/4 cup of shredded Parmesan cheese, divided
- 2 tablespoons of minced onion
- 2/3 cup of light cream
- 1 tablespoon of butter
- 1/8 teaspoon of salt or to taste
- 1 tablespoon of Panko bread crumbs optional
- 1/2 cup of shredded Havarti cheese, divided
- Black pepper to taste

Instructions:
- Preheat your air fryer at 370°F.
- Cook the onion and butter in the pan over medium-low flame till the onion is tender.
- Stir in the garlic for 1 minute or till fragrant. Whisk in the cream, salt, cream cheese, and pepper till smooth. Cook, stirring occasionally, for 1-2 minutes or until the sauce thickens.
- Remove the skillet from the flame and stir in 1/4 cup of Havarti and 2 tablespoons of Parmesan. Add the spinach and mix well.

- Fill a 1 1/2-quart baking dish halfway with the spinach mixture, top with the remaining cheese and bread crumbs, and place in the air fryer basket.
- Cook for around 15-20 minutes.

13. Classic Air Fried Green Bean Casserole

Preparation time: 10 minutes
Cooking time: 30 minutes
Servings: 8
Nutrition facts (Per serving) Calories 167 Fat 10g Protein 5g Carbs 12g
Ingredients:
- 10 1/2 ounces of cream of mushroom soup
- 4 cups of frozen cut green beans, defrosted
- 1/4 teaspoon seasoning salt or to taste
- 1 cup of cheddar cheese sharp, optional
- 1/2 teaspoon black pepper
- 1 teaspoon of soy sauce
- 1 1/2 cups of fried onions crispy
- 1/2 cup of milk low-fat

Instructions:
- Preheat your air fryer at 370°F.
- If using fresh or frozen green beans, cook till they are tender-crisp.
- Combine milk, soup, soy sauce, pepper, green beans, 1 cup of onions, and cheese in a casserole dish. Transfer to the air fryer basket.
- Cook for 20 minutes or till the cheese is bubbling. Remove the pan from the air fryer and mix it well. Return to the air fryer for 5 minutes more, or till browned.

14. Air Fried Ranch Chicken Bacon Casserole

Preparation time: 10 minutes
Cooking time: 20 minutes
Servings: 8
Nutrition facts (Per serving) Calories 469 Fat 31g Protein 38g Carbs 7g
Ingredients:
- 2 lbs. of cooked cubed and shredded chicken breast
- 3/4 cup of ranch dressing
- 8 cooked and chopped slices of bacon
- 1 cup of shredded mozzarella cheese, divided
- 3 garlic cloves minced
- 1 cup of shredded cheddar cheese, divided
- 4 cups of broccoli florets

Instructions:
- Preheat your air fryer at 390°F.
- Bring a pot of water to the boil beside the broccoli. Simmer the vegetables for 1-2 minutes or till they turn vivid green.
- Combine the broccoli, chicken, bacon, garlic, ranch dressing, and half of the shredded cheese in a large-sized mixing bowl. Stir till everything is completely blended. Halfway fill a glass or stoneware casserole dish with the ingredients.
- Top with the remaining mozzarella and cheddar cheese.
- Place the dish in the air fryer basket and cook for approximately 10-15 minutes.

15. Air Fried Zucchini and Halloumi Frittata

Preparation time: 10 minutes
Cooking time: 20 minutes
Servings: 2
Nutrition facts (Per serving) Calories 407 Fat 31.2g Protein 26.7g Carbs 7.8g
Ingredients:
- 1 large grated and squeezed dry zucchini
- 4 ounces of sliced halloumi cheese
- 1 tablespoon of olive oil
- 4 eggs large
- 1 tablespoon of fresh mint chopped
- Salt and black pepper to taste
- 1 tablespoon of fresh dill chopped

Instructions:
- Preheat your air fryer at 370°F.
- Warm the olive oil in a small-sized ovenproof skillet over medium flame. With a touch of salt, cook till zucchini is soft, about 5 minutes. After adding

the chopped mint and dill, cook for another minute. Remove from flame and mix together eggs, salt, and pepper inside a small cup before spreading over the zucchini layer in the skillet.
- Place the frittata in an air fryer basket and top it with halloumi slices. Air fry for around 10-15 minutes before serving.

16. Air Fried Green Chili Casserole

Preparation time: 10 minutes
Cooking time: 30 minutes
Servings: 8
Nutrition facts (Per serving) Calories 137 Fat 9.8g Protein 9.2g Carbs 3.4g
Ingredients:
- 4 lightly beaten eggs
- 2 cans of whole green chili peppers (7 ounces), drained
- 1 1/2 cups of Cheddar cheese shredded, divided
- Salt and pepper to taste
- 1/3 cup of milk

Instructions:
- Preheat your air fryer to 390°F.
- Arrange the bottom of the oiled dish with green chilies. On top, sprinkle with 1/2 cup of shredded cheese. Repeat the layering two more times. Inside a medium-sized mixing cup, whisk together the milk and eggs; season using salt & pepper to taste. Pour the egg mixture over the chilies and cheese.
- Cook for about 15-20 minutes in the air fryer.

17. Air Fried Classic Meatloaf

Preparation time: 10 minutes
Cooking time: 40 minutes
Servings: 4
Nutrition facts (Per serving) Calories 340 Fat 20g Protein 25g Carbs 14g
Ingredients:
- 1 pound of lean ground beef
- 1/4 cup of finely diced onion
- 2 tablespoons of milk
- 1/4 teaspoon of salt and pepper to taste
- 1 clove of minced garlic
- 2 tablespoons of grated parmesan cheese
- 1/2 teaspoon of Italian seasoning
- 1 egg yolk
- 1/2 finely diced green bell pepper
- 1 tablespoon of chopped fresh parsley
- 1/3 cup of seasoned bread crumbs

For the topping:
- 1/4 cup of tomato sauce
- 1/4 cup of chili sauce

Instructions:
- Preheat your air fryer at 350°F.
- Combine all meatloaf ingredients inside a large-sized mixing bowl till well combined. Form the mixture into two small meatloaves, approximately 5" long by 2" wide.
- Inside the air fryer, cook for around 20 minutes.
- Combine the topping ingredients in a small-sized mixing dish. Cook for a further 5-7 minutes after adding the topping. Allow for a 5-minute pause before serving.

18. Air Fryer Feta and Spinach Pie

Preparation time: 10 minutes
Cooking time: 30 minutes
Servings: 6 (1 pie)
Nutrition facts (Per serving) Calories 268 Fat 19g Protein 20.3g, Carbs 5.1g
Ingredients:
- 1 pound of fresh spinach
- 3 ounces of feta cheese crumbled
- 1 tablespoon of butter
- 6 slices of chopped bacon
- 1 pinch of salt
- 12 eggs
- 1/2 diced onion
- 1 pinch of cayenne pepper
- Salt and freshly ground black pepper to taste

Instructions:
- Preheat your air fryer at 370°F.

- Melt butter inside a large-sized oven-safe skillet over a high flame. Toss spinach for 30 seconds in heated butter or till wilted. Squeeze out as much moisture as possible from the spinach. On a cutting board, chop the vegetables.
- Inside a medium-sized mixing bowl, combine eggs, cayenne pepper, salt, and black pepper till well combined.
- Cook the bacon in the same skillet as the spinach for around 5 to 8 minutes, turning occasionally, till the fat has rendered and the bacon is almost crisp. Use tongs and a paper towel to remove excess bacon fat. Reduce the flame to medium and continue to sauté the onion with the bacon and a bit of salt for 5 minutes or till the onion is transparent.
- Cook until the spinach, bacon, and onion are heated, then add the eggs. With a wooden spoon, evenly distribute the spinach into the eggs. On top of the mixture, sprinkle the feta cheese.
- Cook for around 10 to 15 minutes in the air fryer.

19. Air Fried Cloud Bread

Preparation time: 10 minutes
Cooking time: 30 minutes
Servings: 6
Nutrition facts (Per serving) Calories 56 Fat 5g Protein 3g Carbs 1g
Ingredients:
- 3 eggs large, divided
- 1/8 teaspoon of cream of tartar
- 3 tablespoons of cream cheese or 1/3 cup of free or light Greek yogurt

Instructions:
- Preheat your air fryer at 370°F. Line a baking sheet using parchment paper or a Silpat mat.
- Whisk the egg whites and cream of tartar together on high speed till stiff peaks form.
- Whisk together the egg yolks and Greek yogurt (or cream cheese) inside a large-sized mixing dish till creamy. Fold in the remaining egg whites gently till barely blended.
- Divide the egg mixture into 6 equal parts on the prepared pan. Spread it out to a thickness of about 12 inches. Cook in batches as necessary.
- Cook for about 20 minutes or till the top is golden brown. Place on a wire rack to cool completely (at least 60 minutes).

20. Air Fried Creamy Broccoli and Chicken Casserole

Preparation time: 10 minutes
Cooking time: 25 minutes
Servings: 8
Nutrition facts (Per serving) Calories 273 Fat 19g Protein 20g Carbs 6g
Ingredients:
- 20 oz. of broccoli florets
- 1 cup of mozzarella cheese
- 1 lb. of boneless chicken
- 1/2 cup of parmesan cheese
- 1 tablespoon of oil
- 1 cup of Heavy Cream
- 1/2 teaspoon of garlic salt

Instructions:
- Heat the oil in an oven-safe skillet. Cook the chicken till it is golden brown.
- Broccoli florets should be cut into small pieces. Inside a dish, combine with the chicken.
- Combine the parmesan cheese, whipped cream, and garlic salt. Pour the sauce over the broccoli.
- Place the dish in the air fryer basket and cook at 370°F for about 10 minutes. Remove from the air fryer and top with mozzarella cheese, cooking for another 5 minutes or till the cheese is golden brown.

21. Air Fried Healthy Chicken and Veggies

Preparation time: 10 minutes
Cooking time: 20 minutes
Servings: 4

Nutrition facts (Per serving) Calories 230 Fat 10g Protein 26g Carbs 8g

Ingredients:
- 1 pound of chopped chicken breast (bite-size pieces)
- 1 tablespoon of Italian seasoning (or spice blend of choice)
- 1/2 of a teaspoon of each chili powder, garlic powder, salt, pepper
- 2 cloves of minced and crushed garlic
- 1/2 chopped onion
- 1 cup of fresh or frozen broccoli florets
- 2 tablespoons of olive oil
- 1 cup of chopped bell pepper
- 1 chopped zucchini

Instructions:
- Preheat your air fryer to 400°F.
- Cut the veggies and chicken into small bite-size chunks and place them in a large-sized mixing dish. In a mixing bowl, combine the oil and seasoning and toss to coat.
- In the prepared air fryer, cook for 10 minutes, shaking halfway through, or till the chicken and vegetables are blackened, and the chicken is cooked through. You may have to cook them in two or three batches if your air fryer isn't large enough.

22. Air Fried Stuffed Flounder

Preparation time: 10 minutes
Cooking time: 25 minutes
Servings: 8
Nutrition facts (Per serving) Calories 395 Fat 15.7g Protein 52.3g Carbs 8.9g

Ingredients:
- 1 pound of shredded crabmeat
- 3 cloves of minced garlic
- 1/2 chopped green bell pepper, chopped
- Salt and pepper to taste
- 1/4 teaspoon of Cajun seasoning
- 2 tablespoons of softened butter
- 1/3 cup of butter
- 4 pounds of cleaned, rinsed, and dried whole flounder
- 1/2 large minced onion
- 1 bunch of chopped green onions
- 1/2 cup of dry bread crumbs
- 1 stalk of minced celery

Instructions:
- Preheat your air fryer at 370°F.
- Melt the butter in a saucepan over medium-low flame. Combine the green onions, onion, celery, bell pepper, and garlic inside a mixing bowl. Cook, stirring periodically, till the onion softens.
- Remove from the flame and gradually fold in the seasoning, breadcrumbs, shredded crab meat, pepper, and salt.
- Butter the cavity and skin of the flounder. Place in a greased air fryer basket and fill with crab mixture.
- Cook for approximately 15 minutes.

23. Air Fried Crispy Pork Chop Salad

Preparation time: 10 minutes
Cooking time: 20 minutes
Servings: 2
Nutrition facts (Per serving) Calories 526 Fat 37g Protein 5.2g Carbs 34.4g

Ingredients:
- 4 oz. of pork chops, cut into 1" cubes
- 1 tablespoon of cilantro chopped
- 2 oz. of mixed greens
- 1 teaspoon of paprika
- 1/4 cup of ranch dressing
- 1 tablespoon of avocado oil
- 1/2 cup of Colby-Monterey Jack cheese
- 1 peeled, pitted, and diced avocado
- 2 teaspoons of chili powder
- 1/2 teaspoon of garlic powder
- 1 medium diced tomato
- 1/4 teaspoon of onion powder

Instructions:
- Inside a large-sized mixing dish, drizzle avocado oil over the meat. On top, season using garlic powder, chili powder, paprika, and onion powder. Place the pork in an air fryer basket.
- Cook for about 8 minutes at 400°F. When done, the pork will be golden and crispy.

- Inside a large-sized mixing dish, combine the tomato, greens, and crispy pork. Serve with avocado and grated cheese on top. Toss the salad in the ranch dressing to coat it evenly. Garnish with cilantro if desired.

24. Air Fried Cajun Chicken Tenders

Preparation time: 10 minutes
Cooking time: 25 minutes
Servings: 4
Nutrition facts (Per serving) Calories 163 Fat 7.5g Protein 21.2g Carbs 0.7g
Ingredients:
- 1 teaspoon of cumin
- 1/2 teaspoon of black pepper
- 2 teaspoons of paprika
- 1/4 cup of ranch dressing
- 2 teaspoons of avocado oil
- 1/2 teaspoon of cayenne pepper
- 1 teaspoon of ground thyme
- 1/4 teaspoon of salt
- 1 lb. of boneless, skinless chicken breast halves
- 1/2 teaspoon of onion powder

Instructions:
- Inside a small-sized mixing dish, combine all of the seasonings.
- Drizzle avocado oil over the chicken, then generously coat each tender in the spice mixture. Place the tenders in the air fryer basket.
- Cook for about 20 minutes at 375°F. Ranch dressing on the side for dipping.

25. Air Fried Delicious Shrimp Kebabs

Preparation time: 10 minutes
Cooking time: 10 minutes
Servings: 4
Nutrition facts (Per serving) Calories 166 Fat 10.7g Protein 9.5g Carbs 5.4g
Ingredients:
- 1/4 red onion, slice them into 1"-thick squares
- 1 lb. of shrimp
- 1/2 cup of butter melted
- 2 teaspoons of garlic minced
- 1/2 zucchini, slice into 1" cubes
- 1/2 red bell pepper, slice into 1"-thick squares
- Wooden or metal skewers
- 1/2 teaspoon of black pepper
- 1 teaspoon of dried parsley
- 1/2 teaspoon of salt

Instructions:
- Inside a small-sized mixing dish, combine minced garlic, melted butter, dried parsley, salt, and pepper.
- Arrange a shrimp, tomato, zucchini, and onion on a skewer. Rep with the additional ingredients before placing them in the air fryer tray. Then brush the sauce over the kebabs.
- Cook for about 5 minutes at 400°F. Flip the kebabs after half an hour of cooking.
- Brush the kebabs with sauce before serving.

26. Air Fried Chicken Fajitas

Preparation time: 10 minutes
Cooking time: 25 minutes
Servings: 2
Nutrition facts (Per serving) Calories 326 Fat 15.9g Protein 33.5g Carbs 5.2g
Ingredients:
- 1 lb. of thinly sliced chicken breast
- 1 tablespoon of olive or avocado oil
- 1 red pepper, thinly sliced and seeds and stem removed
- 1/2 cup of red onion sliced
- 1 tablespoon of fajita seasoning
- 1 green pepper, thinly sliced and seeds and stem removed

Instructions:
- Inside a large-sized mixing bowl, combine all of the ingredients and swirl well to evenly coat the chicken and vegetables using the oil and seasoning.

- In the air fryer basket, cook the chicken and vegetables for 15 minutes at 350°F, stirring or tossing halfway through with tongs or a fork.

27. Air Fried Chicken Lunch Patties

Preparation time: 10 minutes
Cooking time: 20 minutes
Servings: 4
Nutrition facts (Per serving) Calories 304 Fat 17.4g Protein 32.7g Carbs 0.8g
Ingredients:
- 1/2 teaspoon of garlic powder
- 3 green onions chopped
- 1/2 cup of Provolone shredded
- 1 lb. of ground chicken thigh meat
- 2 oz. of pork rinds finely ground
- 1 tablespoon of dill
- 1/2 cup of shredded Parmesan Cheese
- 1 teaspoon of salt
- 1/4 teaspoon of onion powder
- 1 teaspoon of pepper
- 1 egg large

Instructions:
- Inside a large-sized mixing bowl, combine the ground chicken, onion, cheese, garlic powder, and onion powder. Form the mixture into four patties. Freeze the patties for around 15-20 minutes, or till they firm up.
- Whisk the egg inside a medium-sized mixing cup. Combine the ground pork rinds and dill inside a large-sized mixing bowl.
- Each chicken patty was dipped in the whisked egg and then pushed into the pork rinds to coat completely. Arrange the patties in the air fryer basket.
- Cook for around 12 to 15 minutes at 360°F. Halfway through cooking, flip the pan. Serve hot.

28. Air Fried Fajita-Flavored Flank Steak Rolls

Preparation time: 10 minutes
Cooking time: 30 minutes
Servings: 6
Nutrition facts (Per serving) Calories 439 Fat 26.6g Protein 38g Carbs 2.5g
Ingredients:
- 4 slices of Gouda cheese
- 2 lbs. of flank steak
- 1/4 cup of yellow onion diced
- 1 medium red bell pepper, seeded and cut into strips
- 2 teaspoons of chili powder
- 1 teaspoon of cumin
- 2 tablespoons of avocado oil
- 1/2 teaspoon of garlic powder
- 1 medium green bell pepper, seeded and cut into strips

Instructions:
- Inside a medium-sized skillet over medium flame, sauté the onion, green bell pepper, and red bell pepper. Combine cumin, chili powder, and garlic powder. Cook for around 5-7 minutes, or till the peppers are soft.
- Place the flank steak on a work surface that is flat. Cover the entire rectangle of the steak with the onion and pepper mixture. Just overlap the cheese pieces on top of the onions and peppers.
- Begin rolling the steak with the shortest end facing you, tucking the cheese in as needed. The steak roll is secured using twelve toothpicks, six on each side. Place the steak roll in the air fryer basket.
- Cook for about 15 to 20 minutes at 400°F in the air fryer. Flip the roll halfway through the cooking time.
- Allow the roll to rest for 15 minutes after the timer goes off, then slice into six even slices and serve.

29. Air Fried Leek Egg and Ham Cups

Preparation time: 10 minutes
Cooking time: 15 minutes
Servings: 12
Nutrition facts (Per serving) Calories 153 Fat 10.8g Protein 9.3g Carbs 4.3g
Ingredients:

- 6 eggs
- 2 tablespoons of heavy cream
- 1/4 cup of flour
- 12 deli ham thin slices
- 1 thinly sliced green onion
- 2 cups of beef broth
- 1 thinly sliced leek, white and tender green part only
- 2 tablespoons of butter
- 1 cup of Gruyere cheese shredded
- Salt and pepper to taste

Instructions:
- Preheat your air fryer at 370°F.
- Melt the butter inside a large-sized skillet over a medium-high flame. Cook, frequently turning, till the leek, green onion, pepper, and salt are soft and pliable. Whisk continually as you add the beef broth and flour. Cook the mixture till it is smooth and thick.
- Line each muffin cup with 1 slice of ham to make a cup. 1 tablespoon of the leek mixture should be placed in the bottom of each ham cup. Top with a heaping spoonful of cheese. Press the cheese down lightly with a spoon. Whisk together the eggs and cream inside a large-sized mixing dish. Distribute the egg mixture evenly among the ham cups. Put the cups in the air fryer basket.
- Cook for 10 minutes or till the cups are firm and golden brown.

30. Air Fried Italian Mushroom and Asparagus Frittata

Preparation time: 10 minutes
Cooking time: 25 minutes
Servings: 4
Nutrition facts (Per serving) Calories 194 Fat 12.9g Protein 10.9g Carbs 6.6g
Ingredients:
- 4 eggs
- 1/3 cup of milk
- 1 package (9 ounces) of sliced fresh mushrooms
- 1/3 cup of chicken broth
- 2 tablespoons of extra-virgin olive oil
- 1/2 bunch of asparagus, trimmed and cut into 1-inch pieces
- 3 tablespoons of freshly grated Parmesan cheese, divided
- 1 peeled clove garlic
- Salt and freshly ground black pepper to taste
- 1 tablespoon of chopped fresh parsley

Instructions:
- Preheat your air fryer at 400°F and line an air fryer basket using foil.
- Heat the oil in an oven-safe skillet over medium flame for 1 minute or till the garlic begins to crackle. Cook, stirring occasionally, till the mushrooms and asparagus are cooked, approximately 4 to 5 minutes. Season using salt and add the chicken broth. Remove the garlic.
- Inside a small-sized mixing bowl, combine the milk, eggs, 2 tablespoons Parmesan cheese, parsley, salt, and pepper. Mix gently with the asparagus and mushrooms in the skillet. Cook for approximately 3 minutes or till the eggs start to set. Transfer to an air fryer and sprinkle with remaining 1 tablespoon of Parmesan cheese.
- Cook for around 15 to 20 minutes in the air fryer or until the frittata rises.

Chapter 5: Fish and Seafood Recipes

1. Air Fried Healthy Salmon with Fennel Salad

Preparation time: 10 minutes
Cooking time: 25 minutes
Servings: 4
Nutrition facts (Per serving) Calories 464 Fat 30g Protein 38g Carbs 9g
Ingredients:

- 2 tablespoons of fresh orange juice (from 1 orange)
- 1 teaspoon of kosher salt, divided
- 2/3 cup of 2% reduced-fat Greek yogurt
- 2 tablespoons of fresh dill chopped
- 4 skinless salmon fillets center-cut
- 1 teaspoon of fresh thyme finely chopped
- 4 cups of fennel thinly sliced (from 2 [15-oz.] heads fennel)
- 1 grated clove of garlic
- 2 teaspoons of fresh flat-leaf parsley finely chopped
- 1 teaspoon of fresh lemon juice
- 2 tablespoons of olive oil

Instructions:

- Combine the thyme, parsley, and 1/2 teaspoon salt inside a small-sized mixing dish. Brush the salmon using oil, then generously sprinkle it with the herb mixture.
- Cook 2 salmon fillets in an air fryer basket at 350°F for 10 minutes or till done to preference. Transfer to a hot oven to keep warm. Continue with the remaining fillets in the same manner.
- As the salmon cooks, combine the fennel, yogurt, garlic, orange juice, dill, lemon juice, and the remaining 1/2 teaspoon of salt in a medium-sized mixing bowl. Salmon fillets should be served with a fennel salad on the side.

2. Air Fried Tuna Steak with Sesame Crust

Preparation time: 10 minutes
Cooking time: 15 minutes
Servings: 2
Nutrition facts (Per serving) Calories 280 Fat 10g Protein 42.7g Carbs 1.2g
Ingredients:

- 2 teaspoons of white sesame seeds
- Salt and pepper to taste
- 2 Ahi tuna steaks
- 1 tablespoon of sesame oil
- 2 teaspoons of black sesame seeds
- 1/2 teaspoon of garlic powder

Instructions:

- Finish each tuna steak with a thin layer of oil and a pinch of garlic powder.
- Inside a large-sized mixing bowl, combine the pepper, salt, and sesame seeds, then fully immerse each tuna steak in the mixture. Place tuna steaks in the air fryer basket.

- Cook for about 8 to 10 minutes at 400°F. Flip the steaks halfway through the cooking period.

3. Air Fried Red Pepper Sauce Scallops

Preparation time: 10 minutes
Cooking time: 25 minutes
Servings: 6
Nutrition facts (Per serving) Calories 215 Fat 10.3g Protein 20.7g Carbs 9.9g
Ingredients:
- 2/3 cup of sour cream
- Salt and freshly ground black pepper
- 2 tablespoons of butter
- 1 1/2 lb. of sea scallops
- 2 tablespoons of lemon juice
- 1/4 teaspoon of cayenne pepper
- 4 roasted and deseeded red bell peppers
- 1/4 teaspoon of ground cumin
- 1 tablespoon of chopped fresh parsley, chopped

Instructions:
- Inside a food processor, combine garlic, sour cream, bell peppers, cayenne pepper, cumin, parsley, and lemon juice. Process till a creamy paste forms. Place on a small plate.
- Inside a medium-sized mixing bowl, combine the butter and scallops. Season using salt, pepper, and paprika. Shake well to coat.
- Spread in a baking dish that will fit easily into your air fryer basket.
- Cook for around 12 to 15 minutes at 400°F, turning halfway through.
- Enjoy with red pepper sauce on the side!

4. Air Fried Fish Lentil Patties

Preparation time: 10 minutes
Cooking time: 25 minutes
Servings: 4
Nutrition facts (Per serving) Calories 276 Fat 10.1g Protein 22.7g Carbs 23.4g
Ingredients:
- 1 beaten whole egg
- 1/2 teaspoon of garlic powder
- 1 chopped celery stalk
- 2 tablespoons of chopped cilantro
- 1 cup of cooked lentils
- 1/2 cup of chopped onion
- 1 teaspoon of dried thyme
- Kosher salt and freshly ground black pepper
- 1 medium deseeded and chopped red bell pepper
- 2/3 cup of breadcrumbs
- 10 oz. of cream dory fillets, flaked and steamed
- Olive oil spray

Instructions:
- Place cooked dory fillets on a plate and flake using a fork.
- Inside a large-sized mixing bowl, combine all of the ingredients and season using pepper and salt to taste.
- Make patties with 1/4 cup of ingredients.
- Preheat your air fryer at 380°F.
- Arrange the fish patties in the air fryer basket, so they don't touch. Cook for around 10–15 minutes or till golden brown.

5. Air Fried Scallops with Herbs and Cheese

Preparation time: 10 minutes
Cooking time: 20 minutes
Servings: 4
Nutrition facts (Per serving) Calories 163 Fat 7.4g Protein 20.3g Carbs 3.0g
Ingredients:
- 1 tablespoon of finely chopped parsley
- 2 tablespoons of melted butter
- 1 lb. of fresh sea scallops
- 2 tablespoons of grated parmesan cheese
- 1/2 teaspoon of garlic powder
- 1 tablespoon of finely chopped fresh basil

Instructions:
- Preheat your air fryer at 380°F.

- Inside a small-sized dish, combine the basil, parsley, butter, and garlic powder.
- Brush each scallop using the butter mixture and season using parmesan.
- Place them in the air fryer basket in a single layer, avoiding overcrowding.
- Cook for around 10 to 15 minutes. Repeat with the remaining scallops.

6. Air Fried Mussels with Herb and Lemon

Preparation time: 10 minutes
Cooking time: 15 minutes
Servings: 6
Nutrition facts (Per serving) Calories 207 Fat 10.8g Protein 19.9g Carbs 6.8g
Ingredients:
- 2.2 lbs. of steamed, half shell (top shell removed) mussels
- 1 tablespoon of chopped fresh parsley, chopped
- 1 teaspoon of minced garlic
- 1/4 cup of olive oil
- 1 tablespoon of chopped fresh thyme
- 3 tablespoons of lemon juice
- 1 teaspoon of dried parsley
- Salt and freshly ground black pepper

Instructions:
- Preheat your air fryer at 350°F.
- Inside a mixing bowl, combine all of the ingredients and distribute them in a baking dish large enough to suit your air fryer.
- Cook for approximately 10 minutes. Serve immediately and enjoy.

7. Air Fried Tikka-Style Fish

Preparation time: 10 minutes
Cooking time: 20 minutes
Servings: 6
Nutrition facts (Per serving) Calories 266 Fat 11g Protein 39g Carbs 4g
Ingredients:
- 2 teaspoons of mild chili powder
- 6 tablespoons of plain yogurt
- 2 red snapper or whole sea bream (about 900g/2lb each) or 6 fish steaks like tuna
- 2 teaspoons of turmeric
- 4 crushed or finely grated garlic cloves
- 2 tablespoons of olive oil
- 3 teaspoons of cumin seed
- 2 tablespoons of fresh root ginger finely grated

Instructions:
- If using, slit the entire skin of the fish on both sides using a sharp knife. After seasoning the fish with salt, rub the ginger and garlic all over it.
- Inside a mixing bowl, combine the oil, yogurt, spices, and seasoning. Chill till ready to serve after applying to both the inside and exterior of the fish.
- Cook for about 15 minutes at 400°F, flipping gently halfway through.

8. Air Fried Southwestern Catfish

Preparation time: 10 minutes
Cooking time: 20 minutes
Servings: 4
Nutrition facts (Per serving) Calories 107 Fat 4g Protein 9g Carbs 10g
Ingredients:
- 3 teaspoons of paprika
- 1/4 cup of onion chopped
- 3 teaspoons of chili powder
- 1 to 1-1/2 teaspoons of ground coriander
- 2 tablespoons of white wine vinegar
- 1/2 teaspoon of garlic powder
- 3 medium chopped tomatoes
- 4 (6 ounces each) catfish fillets
- 2 seeded and finely chopped jalapeno peppers
- 3 teaspoons of salt, divided
- 1 to 1-1/2 teaspoons of ground cumin
- 3/4 to 1 teaspoon of cayenne pepper

Instructions:
- Inside a large-sized mixing dish, combine the tomatoes, jalapenos, onion, vinegar, and 1 teaspoon of salt to prepare the salsa.

- After covering, place in the refrigerator for at least 30 minutes.
- Rub the catfish with the remaining salt, paprika, chili powder, cumin, coriander, cayenne pepper, and garlic powder. Moisten a paper towel using cooking oil and lightly coat the air fryer rack with it using long-handled tongs.
- Cook for 12 minutes at 400°F, or till the salmon flakes easily using a fork; halfway during the cooking time, gently flip the fish. Serve with salsa on the side.

9. Air Fried COD with Asparagus

Preparation time: 10 minutes
Cooking time: 15 minutes
Servings: 4
Nutrition facts (Per serving) Calories 141 Fat 3g Protein 23g Carbs 6g
Ingredients:
- 1 pound of trimmed fresh thin asparagus
- 2 tablespoons of lemon juice
- Cod fillets (4 ounces each)
- 1 1/2 teaspoons of lemon zest grated
- 1 pint halved cherry tomatoes
- 1/4 cup of Romano cheese grated

Instructions:
- Brush the cod and asparagus in an air fryer tray using oil. Add the tomatoes, cut side down. Brush lemon juice and lemon zest grated over cod, asparagus and tomatoes.
- Cook for 12 minutes at 400°F or until the fish flakes easily with a fork, sprinkle the grated cheese over and cook for 2 minutes more.

10. Air Fried Parchment Wrapped Orange Tilapia

Preparation time: 10 minutes
Cooking time: 20 minutes
Servings: 4
Nutrition facts (Per serving) Calories 158 Fat 2g Protein 32g Carbs 4g
Ingredients:
- 1/4 cup of orange juice
- 4 teaspoons of orange zest grated
- 1/2 cup of julienned zucchini
- 1/4 teaspoon of cayenne pepper
- 4 (6 ounces each) tilapia fillets
- 1/4 teaspoon of salt
- 1/2 cup of julienned carrot
- 1/4 teaspoon of pepper

Instructions:
- Set aside the orange juice, salt, orange zest, cayenne pepper, and pepper inside a small-sized bowl.
- Place a fish fillet on each of the four 18x12-inch parchment or heavy-duty foil sheets.
- Wrap the parchment paper around the fish. Fold up 3/4 inch of the paper from the bottom inside corner and crimp both layers together to seal. Fold and crimp the edges till you have a half-moon-shaped packet. Proceed with the remaining packets. Fill the air fryer with parchment packets; cook in batches if necessary.
- Cook for about 12 to 15 minutes at 400°F.

11. Air Fried Shrimp and Tomatoes with Sauce

Preparation time: 10 minutes
Cooking time: 15 minutes
Servings: 4 skewers
Nutrition facts (Per serving) Calories 147 Fat 5g Protein 20g Carbs 6g
Ingredients:
- 2 sliced green onions
- 1 pound of peeled and deveined uncooked jumbo shrimp
- 2 teaspoons of 2% milk
- 1/4 cup of plain yogurt
- 2 tablespoons of olive oil
- 1/2 teaspoon of sugar substitute
- 12 cherry tomatoes
- 2/3 cup of arugula fresh
- 2 minced garlic cloves
- 1 teaspoon of cider vinegar
- 1/2 teaspoon of lemon zest grated
- 1/3 cup of lemon juice
- 1 teaspoon of Dijon mustard

- 1/2 teaspoon of salt, divided
- 1/4 teaspoon of pepper

Instructions:
- Inside a large-sized mixing bowl, whisk together the oil, lemon juice, garlic, and lemon zest till thoroughly blended. To coat, toss in the shrimp. Allow for a 10-minute break.
- Combine milk, arugula, green onions, yogurt, vinegar, mustard, sugar substitute, and 1/4 teaspoon salt inside a food processor; process till creamy.
- Season with the remaining salt and pepper, and skewer the shrimp and tomatoes.
- Place the skewers in the air fryer basket. Cook for about 10 minutes at 400°F. Flip the kebabs after half an hour of cooking. Serve with a side of sauce, and enjoy!

12. Air Fried Crispy Salmon Patties

Preparation time: 10 minutes
Cooking time: 15 minutes
Servings: 3
Nutrition facts (Per serving) Calories 373 Fat 25g Protein 33g Carbs 5g
Ingredients:
- 1 teaspoon of fresh dill
- 2 tablespoons of butter
- 1/2 cup of almond flour
- 15 oz. of canned skinless and boneless salmon
- 2 minced green onions
- 1 teaspoon of salt
- 1/2 teaspoon of pepper
- 2 eggs
- 1 teaspoon of fresh parsley

Instructions:
- Incorporate all of the ingredients except the butter inside a mixing bowl and whisk well to combine.
- Using a medium cookie scoop, portion out the mixture. After flattening each ball into a patty, brush it with butter.
- Place the patties in the air fryer basket. Cook for about 8 to 10 minutes at 400°F. Flip each patty carefully halfway through cooking time. The patties will be crispy on the outside after fully cooked.

13. Air Fried Tasty Firecracker Shrimp

Preparation time: 10 minutes
Cooking time: 15 minutes
Servings: 4
Nutrition facts (Per serving) Calories 143 Fat 6.4g Protein 16.4g Carbs 2.8g
Ingredients:
- 1/4 teaspoon of powdered erythritol
- 1 lb. of deveined and peeled Raw Shrimp
- 1/4 cup of full-fat mayonnaise
- 1/4 teaspoon of garlic powder
- 2 tablespoons of sriracha
- 1/8 teaspoon of ground black pepper
- Avocado oil spray
- 1/2 teaspoon of Old Bay seasoning

Instructions:
- Inside a large-sized mixing bowl, coat the shrimp with avocado oil, garlic powder, and Old Bay seasoning. Place the shrimp in the air fryer basket.
- Cook for about 7 minutes at 400°F. Halfway through, flip the shrimp. The shrimp will be brilliant pink when fully cooked.
- In a separate big mixing bowl, combine the powdered erythritol, sriracha, mayonnaise, and pepper. Toss the shrimp with the spicy sauce and serve immediately.

14. Air Fried Creamy Tuna Casserole

Preparation time: 10 minutes
Cooking time: 30 minutes
Servings: 8
Nutrition facts (Per serving) Calories 324 Fat 30g Protein 9g Carbs 7g
Ingredients:
- 2 tablespoons of butter unsalted
- 1 cup of cheddar cheese shredded
- 2 cans of tuna (4.5 oz.)
- 1/2 cup of mozzarella, shredded

- 2 cloves of minced or crushed garlic
- 1 teaspoon of Italian seasoning
- 1/2 teaspoon of black pepper
- 1 pound of broccoli
- 8 oz. of cream cheese
- 1 cup of heavy cream
- 1/2 teaspoon of salt (to taste)

Instructions:
- After chopping the broccoli into little bite-size florets, transfer it to a baking tray. Set aside after fully incorporating the tuna.
- Melt the cream cheese, butter, and cream inside a medium-sized saucepan over medium-high flame, stirring frequently. In a mixing bowl, combine the shredded cheddar cheese, Italian seasoning, garlic, salt, and pepper. To combine, whisk everything together.
- Pour the cheese mixture over the broccoli and tuna mixture and top with shredded mozzarella cheese. Insert the dish into the air fryer basket.
- Cook for about 20 minutes at 390°F or till the top is golden.

15. Air Fried Foil Packed Lobster Tails

Preparation time: 10 minutes
Cooking time: 15 minutes
Servings: 2
Nutrition facts (Per serving) Calories 313 Fat 25.8g Protein 18.1g Carbs 3.3g
Ingredients:
- 4 tablespoons of butter
- 1 clove of grated garlic
- 2 tails of lobster
- Salt and pepper to taste
- 1 teaspoon of lemon zest
- 2 lemon wedges
- 1 teaspoon fresh parsley chopped

Instructions:
- Butterfly lobster tails by cutting longitudinally through the middle of the hard top shells and meat using kitchen shears. Cut to the bottoms of the shells, but not all the way through. Split the tail in half. Place the two halved tails on a layer of aluminum foil in the air fryer basket.
- Melt the butter inside a small-sized saucepan over medium flame. Heat the lemon zest and garlic for 30 seconds or till the garlic is soft. Inside a small-sized bowl, brush 2 tablespoons of the butter mixture onto the lobster tails; seal the foil packets, completely covering the tails. Before serving, season the lobster using pepper and salt.
- Cook for 5 to 7 minutes at 380°F in an air fryer till the lobster meat is opaque. Place the lobster flesh on a platter and top it with the remaining butter saucepan. Garnish with lemon wedges and parsley.

16. Air Fried Scallion Sea Bass

Preparation time: 10 minutes
Cooking time: 20 minutes
Servings: 2-3
Nutrition facts (Per serving) Calories 338.9 Fat 13g Protein 43.7g Carbs 12g
Ingredients:
- 2 tablespoons of lime juice
- 5 teaspoons of olive oil
- 3 tablespoons of soy sauce
- 1 bunch of scallions (white and pale green parts only, cut like match sticks)
- 1 tablespoon of shallot minced
- 12 ounces of sea bass (cut into sections)
- Salt and pepper to season
- 1 tablespoon of minced ginger

Instructions:
- Combine lime juice, soy sauce, ginger, shallot, scallions, and 3 tablespoons of oil, pepper, and salt inside a medium-sized mixing bowl.
- Brush the remaining oil onto the air fryer rack.
- Distribute the sauce over the fish. Save a little for sprinkling toward the end.
- Cook for about 12 minutes at 390°F. When serving, drizzle with the leftover sauce.

17. Air Fried Herb-Crusted Salmon

Preparation time: 10 minutes
Cooking time: 20 minutes
Servings: 8
Nutrition facts (Per serving) Calories 377 Fat 20g Protein 40g Carbs 5g
Ingredients:
- 1 salmon fillet (3 to 4 pounds)
- Salt and pepper to taste
- 2 tablespoons of butter melted
- 1 lemon divided

For the topping:
- 3 cloves of minced garlic
- 2 tablespoons of shredded parmesan cheese
- 1 tablespoon of minced fresh dill
- 3/4 cup of Panko bread crumbs
- One lemon zest
- 2 tablespoons of minced fresh parsley
- 3 tablespoons of melted butter

Instructions:
- Inside a small-sized mixing bowl, combine all of the ingredients. Grease an air fryer basket using cooking spray.
- Rub melted butter all over the salmon, season using pepper and salt, then squeeze half a lemon over the salmon before placing it in an air fryer basket.
- Cook for about 12 minutes at 370°F. When fully cooked, salmon flakes readily with a fork.

18. Air Fried Seafood Gratin

Preparation time: 10 minutes
Cooking time: 30 minutes
Servings: 8
Nutrition facts (Per serving) Calories 397 Fat 19.8g Protein 44.4g Carbs 4.2g
Ingredients:
- 1 pound of crab meat cooked
- 2 cups of hot chicken broth
- 3 tablespoons of butter
- 1 pound of fresh shrimp peeled
- 2 tablespoons of almond flour
- 3 tablespoons of shallots chopped
- 2 cups of shredded provolone cheese
- 1 pound of bay or sea scallops rinsed and drained
- 2 tablespoons of olive oil
- 1/2 cup of Parmesan cheese grated
- 1 can of drained button mushrooms (4 ounces)
- 2 tablespoons of fresh parsley chopped

Instructions:
- Preheat your air fryer at 370°F.
- Cook scallops and shrimp in olive oil inside a large-sized skillet over medium-high flame till firm, about 5 minutes.
- Melt the butter inside a medium-sized saucepan over medium flame. Stir in the flour, then gradually pour in the chicken broth, raising the flame to high and constantly stirring till the sauce thickens. After adding the mushrooms and shallots, cook for around 5 to 10 minutes.
- Layer scallops, crab, and shrimp in the bottoms of oiled baking dishes. Spread the sauce over the seafood and top with the cheese.
- Cook for around 15-20 minutes.

19. Air Fried Pecan-Crusted Tilapia

Preparation time: 10 minutes
Cooking time: 20 minutes
Servings: 4
Nutrition facts (Per serving) Calories 330.4 Fat 12.4g Protein 38.3g Carbs 16.9g
Ingredients:
- 1/2 cup of dry bread crumbs
- 3 tablespoons of almond flour
- 4 (6 ounces) of tilapia fillets
- 1/2 cup of buttermilk (low fat)
- Lemon wedges for garnishing
- 1/4 teaspoon of black pepper
- 1 tablespoon of oil
- 1/2 teaspoon of salt
- 2 tablespoons of chopped pecans
- 1/2 teaspoon of hot sauce
- 1/4 teaspoon of garlic powder

Instructions:
- Combine pecans, breadcrumbs, pepper, garlic, and salt inside a medium-sized mixing bowl.
- Inside a separate medium-sized mixing bowl, combine the spicy sauce and buttermilk. Fill the third dish with flour.
- Coat the fillets in flour, then in buttermilk batter, and finally in breadcrumb mixture.
- Drizzle oil over the fish fillets in an air fryer basket. Cook for around 15 minutes at 390°F. Serve heated with lemon slices on the side.

20. Air Fried Steelhead Trout with Garlic, Lemon and Rosemary

Preparation time: 10 minutes
Cooking time: 15 minutes
Servings: 3-4
Nutrition facts (Per serving) Calories 45.1 Fat 4.6g Protein 0.2g Carbs 1.3g
Ingredients:
- 1 lb. steelhead fillet (with or without skin)
- 1/2 teaspoon of ground black pepper
- 1 lemon zest
- 1 1/2 tablespoons of chopped fresh rosemary
- 1 clove of garlic chopped
- 1 tablespoon of olive and additional for dish greasing
- 1/4 teaspoon of salt
- 1/2 lemon juice

Instructions:
- Preheat your air fryer at 370°F. After lining an air fryer basket using foil, brush it with olive oil.
- Except for the fish, make a paste with all of the ingredients. Place the fish in the paste and season all over with pepper and salt.
- Cook for about 10 minutes, or till the fish is flaky, in a lined air fryer basket.

21. Air Fried Lobster and Crab Stuffed Mushrooms

Preparation time: 10 minutes
Cooking time: 20 minutes
Servings: 8
Nutrition facts (Per serving) Calories 310 Fat 22g Protein 21.9g Carbs 6.9g
Ingredients:
- 1 cup of mozzarella cheese shredded
- 1 pound of fresh mushrooms (stems removed)
- 1 can of crabmeat (6 ounces)
- 1/4 cup of mozzarella cheese shredded
- 1 cup of seasoned croutons crushed
- 3 tablespoons of garlic minced
- 1 pound of cleaned and chopped lobster tail
- 3/4 cup of melted butter(divided)

Instructions:
- Preheat your air fryer at 390°F. 1/4 cup of melted butter should be used to grease a large-sized baking sheet. Place the mushroom caps on a baking sheet in a single layer.
- Combine the remaining 1/2 cup of butter, shredded cheese, smashed croutons, lobster, crab meat, and garlic inside a medium-sized mixing bowl. Filling should be applied evenly to the mushroom caps.
- Air fry for around 10 to 15 minutes, or till the cheese melts and the top is golden brown.

22. Air Fried Shrimp Scampi

Preparation time: 10 minutes
Cooking time: 15 minutes
Servings: 4
Nutrition facts (Per serving) Calories 221 Fat 13g Protein 23g Carbs 1g

Ingredients:
- 1 tablespoon of lemon juice
- 4 tablespoons of butter
- 1 tablespoon of chives chopped
- 2 tablespoons of chicken stock
- 1 lb. of raw shrimp
- 1 tablespoon of minced garlic
- 2 teaspoons of red pepper flakes
- 1 tablespoon of chopped fresh basil

Instructions:
- You should set the temperature of your air fryer at 330 degrees Fahrenheit. Put a 6x3 inch metal pan inside to heat up while you gather the rest of the ingredients.
- Mix the garlic, butter, and red pepper flakes in a heated 6-inch skillet. For 2 minutes, with occasional stirring, the butter should melt.
- Turn on the air fryer and add the ingredients to the pan in the order given, stirring gently between additions.
- Set the timer for 5 minutes and stir once throughout that time. It is at this point that the butter should be melted and liquid.
- Then, using silicone oven mitts, take out the 6-inch pan and lay it aside on the counter to cool for 1 minute. Give it a nice stir at the end of the minute.
- Ideally, at this point, the shrimp would be completely done. If you like, garnish with a few extra basil leaves and enjoy.

23. Air Fryer Southwestern Style Scallops

Preparation time: 10 minutes
Cooking time: 15 minutes
Servings: 4
Nutrition facts (Per serving) Calories 180 Fat 7g Protein 19g Carbs 4g
Ingredients:
- 1/2 cup of chicken broth
- 2 tablespoons of butter, divided
- 1/8 teaspoon of pepper
- 2 teaspoons of chili powder
- 1/2 teaspoon of ground cumin
- 12 sea scallops (around 1 to 1-1/2 pounds)
- 1/4 teaspoon of salt

Instructions:
- Put all the seasonings in one bowl. To season scallops, blot them dry using paper towels and massage them with seasonings.
- Add the scallops to the air fryer basket and brush them with the melted butter.
- At 400 degrees Fahrenheit, food should be ready in about 5 minutes. Flip and continue air frying for another 4–6 minutes or till cooked through.
- Add chicken broth to the cooking pot. Maintain a continual stirring over a medium flame. Bring to a boil, and then decrease the heat to low and simmer till the liquid is reduced by half. Combine the remaining butter by stirring it in till it melts. When the scallops are done cooking, serve them with the sauce you've already made.

24. Air Fried Blue Cheese-Stuffed Shrimp

Preparation time: 10 minutes
Cooking time: 20 minutes
Servings: 2 dozen
Nutrition facts
(Per serving) Calories 43 Fat 2g Protein 6g Carbs 0g
Ingredients:
- 3 ounces of softened cream cheese
- 24 peeled, deveined, and cooked jumbo shrimp
- 1 teaspoon of shallot chopped
- 1/4 cup of blue cheese crumbled
- 2/3 cup of fresh parsley minced, divided
- 1/2 teaspoon of Creole mustard

Instructions:
- In a little food processor or bowl, whip the cream cheese till fluffy. Mix in the remaining parsley, the shallot, the blue cheese, and the mustard.
- Cut the backs of the shrimp open, stopping about half an inch from the bottom. Press the remaining parsley onto the cream cheese filling, then fill.
- At 400 degrees Fahrenheit, food should be ready in about 5 minutes. Air fry for an additional 4–6 minutes, tossing once till the food is fully done.

25. Air Fried Seafood Filled Zucchini

Preparation time: 10 minutes

Cooking time: 25 minutes
Servings: 8
Nutrition facts (Per serving) Calories 197 Fat 6.5g Protein 19.9g Carbs 15g
Ingredients:
- 1 cup of Italian seasoned bread crumbs
- 2 tablespoons of lemon juice fresh
- 4 halved lengthwise zucchini
- 1 cup of Monterey Jack cheese shredded
- 1/2 pound of diced cooked crabmeat
- 2 teaspoons of garlic finely chopped
- 1 1/2 teaspoons of dried oregano
- 1 beaten egg
- 1 1/2 teaspoons of dried basil
- 1 teaspoon of ground black pepper
- 2 tablespoons of fresh lime juice
- 1/2 pound of cooked salad shrimp

Instructions:
- Using a big spoon, scoop off the centers of each zucchini half, retaining the meat.
- Inside a large-sized mixing bowl, combine 1/2 of the leftover zucchini meat, crabmeat, egg, shrimp, and garlic. Whisk in the lime and lemon juices, followed by the Italian-seasoned bread crumbs. To taste, add basil, oregano, and pepper.
- Fill the halves halfway with the shrimp-crabmeat mixture. Place on the air fryer rack.
- Air fry for 15 minutes at 370°F or till done. Cook for another 2 to 3 minutes after adding the cheese.

26. Air Fried Greek-Style Fish Fillets

Preparation time: 10 minutes
Cooking time: 20 minutes
Servings: 8
Nutrition facts (Per serving) Calories 288 Fat 10g Protein 36g Carbs 10g
Ingredients:
- 1/4 teaspoon of garlic powder
- 8 (4 ounces each) tilapia fillets
- 1 tablespoon of lime juice
- 1/4 teaspoon of pepper
- 1/2 teaspoon of paprika
- 1 finely chopped small red onion
- 1/4 cup of plain yogurt
- 1/2 cup of sliced pitted Greek olives
- 2 tablespoons of melted butter
- 1/4 teaspoon of salt
- 1 teaspoon of dill weed
- 1/2 cup of feta cheese crumbled

Instructions:
- Combine the red onion, butter, yogurt, lime juice, dill, paprika, and garlic powder inside a mixing bowl.
- Season the fish in a baking dish with pepper and salt. Layer the cheese and olives on top of the onion mixture in the center of each fillet. Place the dish in the air fryer.
- Cook for around 10 minutes at 390°F in the air fryer. Flip the fillets carefully halfway through cooking.

27. Air Fried Flounder with Stuffing

Preparation time: 10 minutes
Cooking time: 20 minutes
Servings: 6
Nutrition facts (Per serving) Calories 357 Fat 23g Protein 28g Carbs 9g
Ingredients:
For the fish:
- 5 tablespoons of melted butter
- 6 (3 ounces each) flounder fillets
- 1/2 teaspoon of paprika
- 2 tablespoons of lemon juice
- 1 teaspoon of fresh parsley minced
- Salt and pepper to taste

For the stuffing:
- 1 small finely chopped onion
- 1/4 cup of celery finely chopped
- 1 teaspoon of Worcestershire sauce
- 1/2 teaspoon of chives minced
- 1/4 cup of beef broth
- 6 tablespoons of cubed butter
- 1/2 teaspoon of dill weed
- 1/8 teaspoon of cayenne pepper

- 1 pound of shrimp uncooked, peeled, chopped, and deveined
- 1/4 cup of a green pepper finely chopped
- 1 1/2 cups of soft bread crumbs
- 1 teaspoon of pimientos diced, drained
- 1/8 teaspoon of salt

Instructions:
- Inside a large-sized skillet, melt the butter. Cook till the green pepper, onion, and celery are soft. Cook the shrimp, stirring regularly, till they turn pink. Combine the broth, chives, pimientos, Worcestershire sauce, dill, salt, and cayenne pepper. Remove the pan from the flame and stir in the bread crumbs.
- Fill each fillet halfway with stuffing and roll it up. Place the seam side down in an air fryer basket that has been oiled. Brush with a mixture of butter, lemon juice, and spice.
- Cook for around 10 to 15 minutes at 390°F or till the fish is flaky.

28. Air Fryer Cheese Herbed Salmon Frittata

Preparation time: 10 minutes
Cooking time: 25 minutes
Servings: 5
Nutrition facts (Per serving) Calories 217 Fat 12.5g Protein 18.8g Carbs 4.7g
Ingredients:
- 8 oz. of diced and baked salmon
- 1 medium chopped white onion, chopped
- 2 oz. of grated cheddar
- Kosher salt and freshly ground black pepper
- 2 tablespoons of chopped fresh parsley
- 1 clove of minced garlic
- 2 tablespoons of olive oil
- 6 eggs whole
- 2 tablespoons of chopped fresh dill weed

Instructions:
- Preheat your air fryer at 380°F.
- Whisk together 6 eggs, pepper, and salt.
- Inside a medium-sized skillet over medium flame, stir fry onion and garlic in heated oil for about 3 minutes. Cook for another 2 to 3 minutes, stirring in the fish and dill.
- Place the mixture in a baking dish large enough to accommodate your air fryer. Spread the beaten egg mixture over the top and sprinkle with cheddar cheese.
- Place the baking dish in the air fryer basket and cook for around 15 minutes.
- Serve with chopped parsley on top.

29. Air Fried Salmon, Zucchini, and Carrot Patties

Preparation time: 10 minutes
Cooking time: 25 minutes
Servings: 8
Nutrition facts (Per serving) Calories 192 Fat 10g Protein 14g Carbs 11g
Ingredients:
- 16 oz. of drained and flaked pink salmon canned
- Olive oil spray
- 1 medium grated zucchini
- 2 tablespoons of chopped cilantro
- Salt and pepper, to taste
- 1/4 cup of almond flour
- 1 grated carrot
- 3/4 cup of whole-wheat breadcrumbs
- 2 beaten whole eggs
- 1/2 cup of chopped fresh chives

Instructions:
- Combine the salmon, eggs, zucchini, breadcrumbs, carrot, cilantro, almond flour, and chives inside a mixing bowl. Mix in a dusting of pepper and salt to finish.
- Make patties using 1/2 cup of the ingredients and place them in the air fryer basket. Repeat with the remaining mixture. Coat the patties using cooking spray. Cook in small batches.
- Cook for about 15 minutes at 400°F, or till gently browned.

30. Air Fried Prawns with Garlic, Tomato, and Herb

Preparation time: 10 minutes

Cooking time: 20 minutes
Servings: 4
Nutrition facts (Per serving) Calories 210 Fat 9.0g Protein 26.4g Carbs 4.4g
Ingredients:
- 2 tablespoons of olive oil
- 1 cup of halved cherry tomatoes
- 2 tablespoons of fresh parsley
- 1/4 cup of red wine vinegar
- 1 lb. of trimmed tiger prawns
- Salt and freshly ground black pepper
- 1 tablespoon of thinly sliced garlic

Instructions:
- Preheat your air fryer at 380°F.
- Inside a medium-sized mixing bowl, combine the vinegar, olive oil, parsley, and garlic.
- Place the prawns and tomatoes on top. Stir to coat, then season using pepper and salt. Place the prawns and tomatoes in the air fryer basket.
- Cook for 10 to 12 minutes or till the prawns are done. During cooking, turn them once.

Chapter 6:
Vegetable Recipes

1. Air Fried Spicy Stir-Fry Cauliflower

Preparation time: 10 minutes
Cooking time: 30 minutes
Servings: 4
Nutrition facts (Per serving) Calories 93 Fat 3g Protein 4g Carbs 12g
Ingredients:
- 3/4 cup of thinly sliced onion white
- 1 1/2 tablespoons of tamari or gluten-free tamari
- 1 tablespoon of Sriracha
- 1/2 teaspoon of sugar substitute
- 1 head of cauliflower, cut into florets
- 5 finely sliced cloves of garlic
- 1 tablespoon of rice vinegar

Instructions:
- Position the cauliflower in the air fryer. At 350°F. Cook for approximately ten minutes.
- Open the air fryer, remove the container by the handle, shake it, and replace it in the compartment.
- Cook for 10 minutes after adding the sliced onion. Cook for 5 minutes more after adding the garlic.
- Combine the rice vinegar, soy sauce, sugar substitute, Sriracha, pepper, and salt inside a small cup.
- Cook for 5 minutes more after adding the sauce to the cauliflower mixture.

2. Potato and Kale Air Fryer Nuggets

Preparation time: 10 minutes
Cooking time: 50 minutes
Servings: 4
Nutrition facts (Per serving) Calories 40 Fat 0g Protein 3g Carbs 15g
Ingredients:
- 1/4 teaspoon of sea salt
- 4 cups coarsely chopped and loosely packed kale
- 1 teaspoon of extra-virgin olive oil or canola oil
- 1/8 cup of almond milk
- 2 cups of potatoes finely chopped
- 1 minced clove of garlic
- Vegetable oil spray as required
- 1/8 teaspoon of ground black pepper

Instructions:
- Place the potatoes inside a large-sized saucepan of boiling water. Boil and cook the potatoes for approximately 30 minutes or till tender.
- Inside a large-sized skillet over a medium-high flame, heat the oil. Cook till the garlic turns golden brown. Sauté the greens for 2 to 3 minutes. Put everything in a large mixing bowl.
- Drain and place the potatoes inside a medium-sized mixing dish. After adding the salt, milk, and pepper, mash the potatoes using a fork or a potato masher. Inside a

large-sized mixing dish, combine the potatoes and cooked kale. Preheat the air fryer at 390°F for 5 minutes.
- Cut the potato and kale mixture into 1-inch nuggets. Fill the air fryer basket halfway with vegetable oil. Cook for 12 to 15 minutes, shaking every 6 minutes, till golden brown, in the air fryer.

3. Air Fried Asian Green Bean

Preparation time: 10 minutes
Cooking time: 15 minutes
Servings: 2
Nutrition facts (Per serving) Calories 58 Fat 2g Protein 3g Carbs 8g
Ingredients:
- 1 teaspoon of sesame oil
- 8 oz. of fresh green beans
- 1 tablespoon of tamari

Instructions:
- After taking off the ends, cut the green beans in half.
- Fill a resealable plastic bag or a lidded jar with green beans. To blend, shake in the tamari and sesame oil.
- Fill the air fryer basket halfway with green beans. Cook for 10 minutes at 390°F, tossing once halfway through.

4. Air Fried Chipotle Flavored Asparagus

Preparation time: 10 minutes
Cooking time: 15 minutes
Servings: 3
Nutrition facts (Per serving) Calories 15 Fat 0.2g Protein 2.2g Carbs 3.9g
Ingredients:
- Olive oil cooking spray
- 1/2 teaspoon of Salt
- 1 teaspoon of Chipotle powder seasoning
- 10 Asparagus spears whole

Instructions:
- Remove the bottoms of the asparagus spears.
- Coat the bottom of the air fryer basket using nonstick cooking spray. Arrange the asparagus spears in the air fryer basket flat, not overlapping.
- Season the asparagus evenly with the seasonings.
- Cook for about 10 minutes at 350°F.
- The asparagus will be fully cooked at this point, but if you prefer them to crisper, simmer for another 5 minutes.

5. Air Fried Tasty Butternut Squash

Preparation time: 10 minutes
Cooking time: 40 minutes
Servings: 6
Nutrition facts (Per serving) Calories 150 Fat 3g Protein 1g Carbs 10g
Ingredients:
- 1 tablespoon of sugar-free maple syrup
- 8 oz. of steamed and quartered button mushrooms
- 1 cup sliced green onions 3-inch pieces
- 1/4 cup dried cranberries
- 1 tablespoon of olive oil
- 1 tablespoon of balsamic vinegar
- 4 cloves of fresh garlic
- Extra green onion for garnish
- 1 tablespoon of soy sauce
- 4 cups of diced butternut squash diced

Instructions:
- Inside a large-sized mixing dish, combine the green onions, squash, and button mushrooms.
- To make the sauce, follow these steps: Blend or process the soy sauce, olive oil, maple syrup, vinegar, and garlic till smooth.
- Toss the squash mixture in the sauce to coat completely, then transfer it to the air fryer basket. If you're using spray oil, now is the time to use it.
- Cook, shaking every 5 minutes, at 400°F for 25-35 minutes, or till the squash pieces are golden on the exterior and tender on the inside. Toss in the dried cranberries and serve immediately with the extra green onion (if using).

6. Air Fryer Roasted Cauliflower with Cilantro and Lime

Preparation time: 10 minutes
Cooking time: 15 minutes
Servings: 4
Nutrition facts (Per serving) Calories 91 Fat 6.7g Protein 1.3g Carbs 3.8g
Ingredients:
- 3 tablespoons of olive oil
- 2 tablespoons of chili powder
- 6 heaping cups of cauliflower florets (1-1/2-pound cauliflower cut into 1-inch florets)
- Salt to taste
- 3 cloves of garlic
- 1 teaspoon of cumin
- 2 tablespoons of cilantro chopped
- 1 lime medium

Instructions:
- Inside a large-sized mixing bowl, toss cauliflower with olive oil. Chili powder, cumin, garlic powder, and salt are sprinkled over the top. Crush the garlic cloves with the side of a knife.
- Spread seasoned cauliflower and smashed garlic in the air fryer basket. Cook for about 7 minutes at 350°F.
- Cauliflower will be tender and golden around the edges. Place on a serving plate. Cut the lime in half and squeeze the juice over the cauliflower. Garnish with cilantro if desired.

7. Air Fried Cauliflower Cheese Tots

Preparation time: 10 minutes
Cooking time: 30 minutes
Servings: 4
Nutrition facts (Per serving) Calories 181 Fat 9.5g Protein 13.5g Carbs 6.6g
Ingredients:
- 1 egg large
- 1/4 teaspoon of onion powder
- 1.50 oz. 100% cheese crisps
- 1/4 teaspoon of dried parsley
- 1 cauliflower head large
- 1/2 cup of shredded mozzarella cheese
- 1/4 teaspoon of garlic powder

Instructions:
- Fill a big saucepan partly with water and place it on the stovetop with a steamer basket. Allow the water to come to the full boil.
- After removing the center and leaves from the cauliflower, cut them into florets. Carefully place the florets in the steamer basket, then cover.
- Allow the cauliflower to steam for 7 minutes or till soft.
- Remove the steamer basket from the pan and set it aside for 10 minutes to cool. Squeeze as much excess moisture as possible over the sink using cheesecloth or a clean dish towel. If you don't extract enough water, the tots will become soggy.
- Combine the mozzarella, cauliflower, cheese crisps, garlic powder, egg, parsley, and onion powder inside a food processor. Process on low for 1 minute, scraping down the edges as needed. The mixture should be somewhat moist but keep its shape when molded.
- To make a tot, take 2 teaspoons of the mixture and roll it into a ball with your hands. Repeat with the remaining mixture. Insert a piece of parchment paper into the bottom of your air fryer basket.
- Place the tots in the basket, making sure to weigh down each edge with a tot; otherwise, the parchment will blow and the tots will not cook evenly.
- Cook for around 12 minutes at 320°F; turn the tots halfway through.

8. Air Fried Root Vegetables

Preparation time: 10 minutes
Cooking time: 25 minutes
Servings: 6
Nutrition facts (Per serving) Calories 242 Fat 7g Protein 3g Carbs 43g
Ingredients:

- 3 pounds of assorted root vegetables (chopped into 1 1/2-inch piece)
- 1 teaspoon of salt
- Cracked pepper to taste
- 4 cloves of minced garlic
- 1 teaspoon of dried rosemary
- 3 tablespoons of olive oil
- 1 red onion large (chopped into 1 1/2-inch piece)

Instructions:
- Preheat your air fryer for 3 minutes at 400°F. Combine all of the vegetables, onion, and garlic, minced, inside a large-sized mixing dish. In a mixing dish, combine the olive oil, rosemary, ground pepper, and salt.
- Mix till the vegetables are well covered (use your hands to toss the vegetables).
- Distribute evenly in the air fryer basket.
- Cook for approximately 8 minutes. After tossing the vegetables, cook for another 6 to 8 minutes.

9. Air Fryer Tasty Zucchini Casserole

Preparation time: 10 minutes
Cooking time: 30 minutes
Servings: 8
Nutrition facts (Per serving) Calories 84 Fat 5g Protein 2g Carbs 6g
Ingredients:
- 1 pound of Roma tomatoes (cut into 1/4 inch slices)
- 1 1/2 pounds of zucchini (cut into 1/2 inch slices)
- Fresh basil and parsley for serving
- 1 1/2 tablespoons of olive oil
- 1 clove of minced garlic
- 1/2 teaspoon of Italian seasoning

For the topping:
- 2 tablespoons of melted butter
- 1/2 chopped onion
- 2/3 cup of shredded mozzarella cheese
- 1/4 cup of parmesan cheese fresh
- 1 tablespoon of olive oil
- 1/4 cup of whole wheat bread crumbs

Instructions:
- Preheat your air fryer at 370°F.
- Cook the onion in olive oil till soft, about 5 minutes, then leave aside to cool.
- Cut tomatoes into slices and set them on paper towels for 2 to 3 minutes to absorb liquid.
- Combine the zucchini, olive oil, Italian seasoning, and garlic in a mixing bowl. Season with pepper and salt and toss thoroughly to coat.
- Arrange the tomatoes and zucchini in a baking dish. Air fry for about 10 minutes.
- To prepare the topping, whisk together all of the ingredients (including onions from step first and mix well).
- Spread the topping over the zucchini and bake for another 10 minutes or until soft. Serve the casserole hot, garnished with fresh herbs.

10. Healthy and Tasty Air Fried Broccoli Tots

Preparation time: 10 minutes
Cooking time: 20 minutes
Servings: 20 tots
Nutrition facts (Per serving) Calories 26 Fat 1g Protein 1g Carbs 3g
Ingredients:
- 2 cups or 12 ounces of frozen broccoli or uncooked
- 1/3 cup of cheddar cheese
- 1/2 teaspoon of pepper
- 1 egg large
- 1/3 cup of Italian breadcrumbs
- 2 tablespoons of parsley (rosemary or cilantro)
- 1/4 cup of yellow onion diced
- 1/3 cup of panko breadcrumbs
- 1/2 teaspoon of salt

Instructions:
- Preheat the air fryer at 400°F.
- Boil the broccoli for 1 minute, then drain and rinse with cool tap water.
- Chop the broccoli finely and combine it with the egg, onions, cheddar, seasonings,

and breadcrumbs. Gently press 1.5 tablespoons of ingredients into a tot shape using your hands using an ice- or food scoop. Place them in a greased air fryer basket and spray using cooking spray.
- Cook for around 10-15 minutes, shaking the pan halfway through the air frying.

11. Air Fried Celery Sticks

Preparation time: 10 minutes
Cooking time: 20 minutes
Servings: 6
Nutrition facts (Per serving) Calories 162 Fat 4.2g Protein 8.0g Carbs 23.0g
Ingredients:
- 4 stalks of celery, trimmed and slice into 3-inch pieces
- 1/2 cup of almond flour for dusting
- 2 eggs whole
- 1/2 teaspoon of Kosher salt
- 1 teaspoon of lemon pepper
- 1/4 cup of grated parmesan cheese
- 1 cup of whole-wheat breadcrumbs
- 1/2 teaspoon of garlic powder
- Cooking oil spray
- 1/2 teaspoon of onion powder

Instructions:
- Preheat your air fryer at 400°F.
- Set aside the eggs after thoroughly mixing them using salt and lemon pepper inside a small-sized dish.
- Inside a separate bowl, combine the almond flour, breadcrumbs, parmesan, onion powder, and garlic powder.
- Each stick should be dipped in the egg and then in the breadcrumbs. Roll in the breadcrumb mixture till completely covered.
- Place the celery in the air fryer basket and coat using oil. Cook in batches if required; do not overcrowd the pan.
- Cook for about 15 minutes or till golden brown, turning once halfway through.

12. Air Fried Ratatouille

Preparation time: 10 minutes
Cooking time: 30 minutes
Servings: 4
Nutrition facts (Per serving) Calories 153 Fat 7.7g Protein 3.9g Carbs 21.1g
Ingredients:
- 1 tablespoon of garlic
- 1 tablespoon of herbs de Provence
- 2 tablespoons of olive oil
- 1 zucchini medium
- 2 yellow peppers medium
- 1 eggplant medium
- 3 tomatoes medium
- 1 tablespoon of vinegar
- Salt and pepper to taste
- 1 onion medium

Instructions:
- Preheat your air fryer at 400°F.
- With a sharp knife, cut the peppers, tomatoes, onions, zucchini, and eggplant into 2-inch chunks. Garlic must be minced.
- Inside a mixing dish, combine the garlic, veggies, and herbs de Provence. Season using pepper and salt to taste.
- Drizzle with extra virgin olive oil and balsamic vinegar to taste. Toss to coat evenly.
- In an oven-safe dish that fits inside the Air Fryer basket, combine the ingredients and bake for 15 minutes. Stir once during the cooking process.

13. Air Fried Vegetable Tofu

Preparation time: 10 minutes
Cooking time: 25 minutes
Servings: 4
Nutrition facts (Per serving) Calories 192 Fat 11.7g Protein 11.8g Carbs 11.5g
Ingredients:
- 8 oz. (250 g) of asparagus, make small pieces
- 3 tablespoons of rice wine vinegar
- Kosher salt and pepper, to taste
- 2 tablespoons of soy sauce
- 16 oz. (450 g) of firm tofu, make cubes
- 2 leeks, diagonally sliced
- 1 teaspoon of Worcestershire sauce
- 2 tablespoons of peanut oil

- 1 teaspoon of minced garlic

Instructions:
- Preheat your air fryer at 400°F.
- In a medium mixing bowl, combine the peanut oil, rice wine vinegar, soy sauce, Worcestershire sauce, and garlic.
- In a mixing bowl, combine the leeks, tofu, and asparagus. Toss to coat evenly. Season with salt and pepper to taste.
- Place in a baking dish large enough to fit in your Air Fryer basket. Cook for approximately 15 minutes.

14. Air Fried Okra

Preparation time: 10 minutes
Cooking time: 20 minutes
Servings: 4
Nutrition facts (Per serving) Calories 75.1 Fat 5.3 g Protein 1.9 g Carbs 7g
Ingredients:
- 1/4 teaspoon of ground cumin
- 1/2 teaspoon of smoked paprika
- 12 ounces of small okra
- 1/2 teaspoon of salt
- 4 lemon wedges (for garnishing)
- 1/4 teaspoon of cayenne pepper
- 1 1/2 tablespoons of olive oil
- 1/4 teaspoon of ground coriander

Instructions:
- Coat the okra using olive oil.
- Inside a small-sized bowl, combine cumin, coriander, cayenne pepper, paprika, and salt; toss okra evenly in the spice mixture.
- Place the coated okra in an air fryer basket and cook for around 14 to 15 minutes at 390°F, flipping halfway through.
- Serve immediately with lemon wedges squeezed over each portion.

15. Air Fried Broccoli Casserole

Preparation time: 10 minutes
Cooking time: 25 minutes
Servings: 6 to 8
Nutrition facts (Per serving) Calories 272 Fat 20.8g Protein 7.5g Carbs 13.9g
Ingredients:
- 1/2 cup of mayonnaise
- 1 package of frozen chopped broccoli (16 ounces)
- 1/2 cup of processed cheese sauce
- 2 beaten eggs
- 1/2 cup of whole wheat bread crumbs
- 1 can of condensed cream of mushroom soup (10.75 ounces)

Instructions:
- Inside a casserole dish, combine broccoli, processed cheese, mayonnaise, mushroom soup, and eggs. Mix everything together, then coat using bread crumbs and place the dish in the air fryer basket.
- Cook for around 18 to 20 minutes at 375°F in an air fryer.

16. Air Fried Greek-Style Stuffed Eggplant

Preparation time: 10 minutes
Cooking time: 25 minutes
Servings: 2
Nutrition facts (Per serving) Calories 291 Fat 18.7g Protein 9.4g Carbs 11.8g
Ingredients:
- 2 tablespoons of red bell pepper diced
- 1/4 cup of artichoke hearts chopped
- 1 eggplant large
- 2 tablespoons of olive oil extra virgin
- 1/2 cup of grated hard aged cheese
- 1/4 onion organic medium
- 1/2 teaspoon of oregano
- 1 cup of fresh spinach
- 1/2 teaspoon of paprika
- Salt and pepper to taste
- 1/2 teaspoon of cinnamon

Instructions:
- Cut the eggplant in half lengthwise, then scoop out the skin, leaving enough within to keep the shell intact. Scoop out the eggplant, cut it, and set it aside.
- Inside a medium-sized skillet over medium flame, combine the onion and oil. Sauté for 3 to 5 minutes or till onions soften. Combine the eggplant, spinach, artichokes,

bell pepper, and all of the spices in a mixing bowl. Cook for another 5 minutes or until the peppers soften and the spinach wilts. Turn off the flame.
- Stuff the eggplant with the mixture and place it in the air fryer basket.
- Cook for around 15 to 20 minutes at 375°F in an air fryer.

17. Air Fryer Roasted Veggie Bowl

Preparation time: 10 minutes
Cooking time: 25 minutes
Servings: 6
Nutrition facts (Per serving) Calories 81 Fat 4g Protein 3g Carbs 10g
Ingredients:
- 1 tablespoon of olive oil
- 1/2 cup of sliced baby zucchini
- 1 small sliced onion
- 1 cup of broccoli florets
- 1/4 cup of balsamic vinegar
- 1 cup of cauliflower florets
- 1/2 cup of baby carrots
- 1 tablespoon of garlic minced
- 1/2 cup of sliced yellow squash
- 1 teaspoon of red pepper flakes
- 1/2 cup of mushrooms sliced
- 1 teaspoon of sea salt
- 1/4 cup of Parmesan cheese
- 1 teaspoon of black pepper

Instructions:
- Preheat your air fryer for 3 minutes at 400°F.
- Inside a large-sized mixing bowl, combine the balsamic vinegar, olive oil, salt, garlic, pepper, and red pepper flakes. Combine all of the ingredients, then add the veggies and stir to coat evenly.
- Vegetables should be placed in the Air Fryer basket. Cook for approximately 8 minutes.
- After tossing the vegetables, cook for another 6 to 8 minutes.
- Cook for 1- 2 minutes after adding the cheese.

18. Air Fryer Roasted Loaded Broccoli

Preparation time: 10 minutes
Cooking time: 15 minutes
Servings: 4
Nutrition facts (Per serving) Calories 133 Fat 9g Protein 8g Carbs 7g
Ingredients:
- 12 oz. of fresh Broccoli Florets
- 1 chopped green onion
- 1/2 cup of shredded cheddar cheese
- 2 slices of crisp bacon crumbled
- 1/4 cup of sour cream
- 1 tablespoon of olive oil

Instructions:
- Place the broccoli in the air fryer basket and drizzle with olive oil.
- Cook for about 10 minutes at 350°F.
- Toss the basket two or three times throughout cooking to avoid burnt spots.
- When the broccoli's ends start to crisp, remove it from the frying. Garnish with green onion, shredded cheese, sour cream, and bacon crumbles.

19. Air Fried Asparagus with Cheese Sauce

Preparation time: 10 minutes
Cooking time: 15 minutes
Servings: 8
Nutrition facts (Per serving) Calories 113 Fat 7.3g Protein 7.6g Carbs 4.9g
Ingredients:
- 1 cup of cream half-and-half
- 1/2 teaspoon of ground mustard
- 1 cup of mozzarella cheese shredded
- 2 teaspoons of cornstarch
- 1 pound of trimmed fresh asparagus
- 1/4 teaspoon of red pepper flakes
- 1 teaspoon of Italian seasoning
- 1/2 cup of Parmesan cheese grated

Instructions:
- Inside a small-sized baking dish, arrange the asparagus.

- Half-and-half, Italian seasoning, ground mustard, mozzarella cheese, red pepper flakes, cornstarch, and parmesan cheese should all be combined. Spread the mixture over the asparagus in a baking dish.
- Cook for about 10 to 12 minutes at 350°F in the air fryer.

20. Air Fried Cheesy Herbed Cauliflower Quinoa Casserole

Preparation time: 10 minutes
Cooking time: 35 minutes
Servings: 5
Nutrition facts (Per serving) Calories 239 Fat 12.2g Protein 16g Carbs 16.1g
Ingredients:
- 1/4 cup of parsley
- 4 cups (480 g) cauliflower florets
- 2/3 cup of crumbled cottage cheese
- Sea salt and freshly ground black pepper
- 4 oz. of grated mozzarella cheese
- 2 tablespoons of grass-fed butter
- 1 cup of low-fat milk
- 4 oz. of grated mozzarella cheese
- 2/3 cup of cooked quinoa

Instructions:
- Preheat your air fryer at 360°F.
- Inside a saucepan, bring water to the boil. After adding the cauliflower florets, cook for 1 minute. Drain and set aside.
- In a mixing bowl, combine cauliflower florets, butter, parsley, milk, quinoa, and cottage cheese. Season with salt and pepper to taste. Mix everything together thoroughly.
- Cook in batches if necessary. Transfer the contents to a casserole dish that will fit in the Air Fryer cooking basket. Top with the mozzarella.
- Place the casserole dish in the Air Fryer's cooking basket.
- Cook for 20-25 minutes, or till the cheese is melted and the dish is thoroughly cooked.

21. Air Fried Eggplant Tomato Casserole

Preparation time: 10 minutes
Cooking time: 30 minutes
Servings: 4
Nutrition facts (Per serving) Calories 209 Fat 11.1g Protein 8.9g Carbs 23.7g
Ingredients:
- 4 eggplants, cut into 1/2-inch rounds
- 1/2 cup of grated Parmesan cheese
- 1 teaspoon of minced garlic
- 2 tablespoons of olive oil
- 1 cup of tomato puree
- 2 tablespoons of chopped fresh oregano
- 1 sliced onion
- 2 cups of cherry tomatoes, slice into quarters
- 1/4 cup of chopped fresh basil, chopped
- Salt and freshly ground black pepper

Instructions:
- Inside a medium-sized skillet over medium flame, heat the oil. For 3 minutes, sauté the onion and garlic.
- Cook for 5 minutes on low flame, stirring in the eggplant, tomato puree, and cherry tomatoes. Season to taste using salt and pepper. Place in a baking dish large enough to suit your air fryer. Finish with Parmesan cheese and basil leaves.
- Cook for around 20 minutes at 360°F.

22. Air Fried Sweet Corn Custard

Preparation time: 10 minutes
Cooking time: 40 minutes
Servings: 6
Nutrition facts (Per serving) Calories 210 Fat 14.6g Protein 8.3g Carbs 13.8g
Ingredients:
- 2 eggs
- 1 1/2 cups of half and half cream
- 1 tablespoon of butter, divided
- 1/2 cup of cold milk
- 3 egg yolks
- 1/4 teaspoon of paprika
- 2 cups of whole sweet corn kernels
- 1/2 teaspoon of salt

Instructions:

- Preheat your air fryer at 325°F.
- Lightly grease six ramekins in butter, then place them in a 2-inch deep baking dish.
- Inside a large-sized saucepan, mix together the cream, corn, salt, and paprika. Bring to a simmer and then remove from the flame; stir in the milk and butter.
- Add the corn mixture to a food processor and process. Cook till the mixture is creamy.
- Whisk the egg yolks and entire eggs together until smooth and creamy. After a few minutes, gradually whisk in the heated corn mixture.
- Divide the prepared mixture among the ramekins evenly. Bring some water to a boil and then pour it halfway up the dish. Place the dish in the air fryer.
- Cook for 30 minutes or till the custard is firm.

23. Air Fried Vegetables and Cheese Skewers

Preparation time: 10 minutes
Cooking time: 25 minutes
Servings: 6
Nutrition facts (Per serving) Calories 130 Fat 10.3g Protein 4.8g Carbs 6.2g
Ingredients:
- 1 cup of diced feta cheese
- 2 cups of cherry tomatoes
- 1/2 teaspoon of paprika
- 1 medium of zucchini, cut into wedges
- 1/2 teaspoon of dried thyme
- 2 tablespoons of olive oil
- Salt and freshly ground black pepper
- 1 red bell pepper medium, slice into 2-inch pieces
- 2 tablespoons of lemon juice

Instructions:
- Preheat your air fryer at 400°F.
- Combine the olive oil, lemon juice, thyme, and paprika inside a mixing bowl.
- Finally, add the vegetables and season using salt and pepper to taste. Shake to evenly coat.
- Arrange the feta cheese and veggies on bamboo skewers.
- Cook the veggie skewers in the air fryer basket for around 15 minutes.

24. Air Fried Vegetable Frittata

Preparation time: 10 minutes
Cooking time: 35 minutes
Servings: 6
Nutrition facts (Per serving) Calories 315 Fat 18.7g Protein 18.3g Carbs 19.2g
Ingredients:
- 1 large chopped leek (white part only)
- 1/2 teaspoon of ground black pepper
- 4 ounces of goat-milk feta cheese crumbled, divided
- 1 pinch of cayenne pepper
- 2 tablespoons of olive oil
- 1 cup of baby spinach
- 1 1/2 cups of sliced zucchini (cut in 1/2-inch slices)
- 12 eggs large
- 1 1/2 cups of sliced potatoes cooked
- 1 jalapeno pepper, diced and seeded
- 1 1/2 cups of asparagus (cut into 1/2-inch pieces)
- 1 teaspoon of salt

Instructions:
- Preheat your air fryer at 360°F.
- Inside a medium-sized skillet, heat the oil and sauté the leeks with a bit of salt, stirring periodically, till translucent and smooth, about 5 to 6 minutes. Add the zucchini and jalapeno, along with a pinch of salt, to the pan. Cook for about 5 minutes or till the zucchini turns a light green color. Then add the asparagus and cook for 1 to 2 minutes before adding the spinach and seasoning with salt. Cook for another 1 minute or till the spinach has wilted. Cook for 5 minutes more after adding the cooked potatoes.
- Fill a dish with 12 large eggs. Season to taste with salt, pepper, and cayenne pepper. Whisk for 1 minute. Spread the egg mixture into the skillet with the vegetables on medium flame. Stir in 3 ounces of goat

cheese, then top with the remaining cheese. Turn off the stove.
- Cook in the air fryer for around 18 to 20 minutes or till the frittata is set.

25. Air Fried Tasty and Crispy Artichoke Fries

Preparation time: 10 minutes
Cooking time: 20 minutes
Servings: 4
Nutrition facts (Per serving) Calories 120 Fat 5g Protein 2g Carbs 14g
Ingredients:
- 1 cup of Almond Flour
- 1/2 teaspoon of Paprika
- 14 oz. of quartered Artichoke Hearts
- 1/4 teaspoon of Black Pepper, or to taste
- 1 cup of Plant-Based Milk Unsweetened
- 1 1/2 cups of whole wheat bread crumbs
- 3/4 teaspoon of Salt
- 1/2 teaspoon of Garlic Powder
- 1/4 teaspoon of Salt

Instructions:
- Drain and quarter the canned artichoke hearts.
- Arrange the halved Artichoke Hearts in a row on half of a large, clean towel. To extract moisture, fold down the other half of the towel on the quarter's top and gently push down. While you prepare the dry and wet ingredients, allow the artichokes to dry further in the towel.
- Inside a small-sized bowl with a large rim, combine all of the ingredients to produce the wet mixture. The mixture should be slightly thicker than the pancake batter.
- Prepare the Dry Mixture in a separate rimmed broad small-sized dish.
- Dip each artichoke quarter into the Wet Liquid with separate hands, shake out the excess mixture, and then coat evenly in the Dry Mixture. Rep with the rest of the artichoke bits.
- In an air fryer, cook for around 10 to 15 minutes at 340°F. Working in batches provides some "breathing room" between tasks.

26. Air Fried BBQ Flavored Soy Curls

Preparation time: 10 minutes
Cooking time: 20 minutes
Servings: 2
Nutrition facts (Per serving) Calories 136 Fat 3g Protein 7g Carbs 18g
Ingredients:
- 1/4 cup of BBQ sauce
- 1 cup of warm water
- 1 teaspoon of vegetarian Better Than Bouillon
- 1 cup of Soy Curls

Instructions:
- In a tub, soak Soy Curls in water and bouillon for 10 minutes. Squeeze off as much water as possible from the soy curls in a strainer.
- Transfer the moistened Curls to a mixing bowl and shred them by hand like string cheese.
- Air fry the Soy Curls for 3 to 5 minutes at 400°F. Remove from the air fryer and return to the mixing bowl. Stir in the BBQ sauce. Make sure to equally cover all of the curls. Replace the air fryer in its original location. Air fry for 5 minutes at 400°F, stopping twice to shake the pan.

27. Air Fried Parmesan-Herb Tomatoes

Preparation time: 10 minutes
Cooking time: 20 minutes
Servings: 6
Nutrition facts (Per serving) Calories 53 Fat 3g Protein 2g Carbs 3g
Ingredients:
- 3 tablespoons of fresh herbs (oregano, parsley, and basil)
- 3/4 cup of whole wheat fresh bread crumbs
- Salt and black pepper (according to taste)
- 1/4 cup of parmesan cheese grated
- 1 tablespoon of olive oil
- 3 large red ripe tomatoes (halved)

- 1 clove of minced garlic

Instructions:
- Inside a small-sized mixing bowl, combine the cheese, breadcrumbs, olive oil, herbs, pepper, and salt. Toss till fully combined.
- Spread the sliced tomatoes in a prepared air fryer basket, season using pepper and salt, and top with the breadcrumb mixture.
- Cook for about 8 to 10 minutes at 400°F. Flip the slices halfway through. Serve immediately.

28. Air Fryer Roasted Basil Red Peppers

Preparation time: 10 minutes
Cooking time: 20 minutes
Servings: 6
Nutrition facts (Per serving) Calories 84 Fat 5.8g Protein 1g Carbs 5.7g
Ingredients:
- 2 tablespoons of balsamic vinegar
- 6 halved cherry tomatoes
- 2 tablespoons of rinsed and drained capers
- 3 leaves of fresh thyme sprigs
- A handful of fresh basil leaves
- 3 red peppers large
- 2 crushed garlic cloves
- 3 tablespoons of extra-virgin olive oil

Instructions:
- Remove the seeds from the pepper by cutting it in half lengthwise.
- Spread the garlic, thyme leaves, tomatoes, and capers inside the nonstick baking tray between the red peppers, cut side up. Season with salt and pepper before placing the tray in the air fryer basket.
- Cook for about 10 minutes at 370°F. After 10 minutes, sprinkle balsamic vinegar over the dish and air fry for another 5 minutes or till soft and caramelized. Serve with fresh basil on top.

29. Air Fryer Seasoned Eggplant

Preparation time: 10 minutes
Cooking time: 20 minutes
Servings: 6
Nutrition facts (Per serving) Calories 54 Fat 3.7g Protein 2.4g Carbs 3.2g
Ingredients:
- 1 tablespoon of olive oil
- 3 sliced tomatoes
- Cooking spray
- 1 eggplant (cut into 1/2-inch-thick round slices)
- Salt to taste
- 1/3 cup of Parmesan cheese grated
- 1 teaspoon of oregano
- Black pepper to taste

Instructions:
- Cover each eggplant slice with a tomato slice in an air fryer basket. Drizzle the eggplant and tomato with olive oil, season with salt, oregano, and pepper, and top with a thick layer of parmesan cheese.
- Cook for about 15 minutes at 390°F or till the cheese begins to brown.

30. Air Fried Eggplant with Cherry Tomatoes and Herbs

Preparation time: 10 minutes
Cooking time: 35 minutes
Servings: 4
Nutrition facts (Per serving) Calories 198 Fat 8.7g Protein 5.1g Carbs 28.5g
Ingredients:
- 1/3 cup of tomato puree
- 2 cups of cherry tomatoes, slice into quarters
- Salt and freshly ground black pepper
- 2 minced cloves of garlic
- 1/4 cup of chopped fresh flat-leaf parsley
- 3 eggplants, sliced into 1/2-inch wedges
- 2 tablespoons of chopped fresh oregano
- 3 tablespoons of olive oil

Instructions:
- Preheat your air fryer at 400°F.
- Inside a small-sized mixing dish, combine the tomato puree, olive oil, garlic, oregano, and parsley. Now add the eggplant and shake well to coat.

- Place them in a baking dish large enough to accommodate your air fryer. Spread with cherry tomatoes and season using pepper and salt.
- Cook for around 20 to 25 minutes or till the desired doneness is reached.

Chapter 7: Beef Recipes

1. Air Fried Sirloin Steak with Thyme and Garlic

Preparation time: 10 minutes
Cooking time: 20 minutes
Servings 4
Nutrition facts (Per serving) Calories 274 Fat 12.2g Protein 34.5g Carbs 0.7g
Ingredients:
- 4 steaks of sirloin

For the steak rub:
- 1 teaspoon of minced garlic
- 2 tablespoons of steak sauce low-sodium
- 1/4 teaspoon of kosher salt
- 1 tablespoon of chopped fresh thyme
- 1/2 teaspoon of ground coriander seeds
- 2 tablespoons of olive oil
- 1/4 teaspoon of freshly ground black ground pepper

Instructions:
- Preheat your air fryer at 360°F.
- Combine all of the steak rub ingredients inside a mixing bowl. Place the steak on top of the mixture and rub it in. Allow to stand in the refrigerator for about 30 minutes, covered.
- Cook the steaks in the air fryer basket for around 12 to 15 minutes.

2. Air Fried Grilled Spiced Steak and Vegetables

Preparation time: 10 minutes
Cooking time: 15 minutes
Servings 4
Nutrition facts (Per serving) Calories 285 Fat 13.6g Protein 32.4g Carbs 8.8g
Ingredients:
- 1/4 teaspoon of salt
- 4 sirloin beef steak
- 1/2 teaspoon of paprika
- 1 red bell pepper medium, cut into strips
- 1/4 teaspoon of freshly ground black pepper
- 4 tablespoons of olive oil, divided
- 1 bunch of trimmed asparagus
- 1/2 teaspoon of the ground cumin
- 1 medium sliced red onion

Instructions:
- Preheat your air fryer at 400°F.
- Combine ground cumin, 2 tablespoons of olive oil, salt, paprika, and pepper inside a small-sized dish. Rub the mixture over the steak to coat both sides. Place them aside.
- Spread the remaining olive oil over the onion, bell pepper, and asparagus inside a large-sized dish, and season using pepper and salt. To coat, lightly toss the ingredients.
- In the air fryer basket, layer the vegetables first, then the steaks, and cook for 10 to 15 minutes on each side.

3. Air Fried Carne Asada

Preparation time: 10 minutes
Cooking time: 20 minutes
Servings 4

Nutrition facts (Per serving) Calories 351 Fat 14g Protein 28g Carbs 28g
Ingredients:
- 1 pound of flank steak

For the Marinade:
- 1/4 cup of fresh lime juice
- 3 cloves of garlic
- 1 tablespoon of soy sauce
- 2 tablespoons of vegetable oil
- 1 teaspoon of cumin
- 1/3 cup of orange juice
- 1 jalapeno halved and seeded

Instructions:
- Preheat your air fryer at 400°F.
- Blend all marinade ingredients in a blender till smooth. Spread the mixture over the flank steak and leave to marinade for 4 hours or overnight.
- Cook the steaks in the air fryer basket for about 20 to 25 minutes, flipping halfway through.

4. Air Fried Russian Beef

Preparation time: 10 minutes
Cooking time: 20 minutes
Servings 6
Nutrition facts (Per serving) Calories 530 Fat 41g Protein 33g Carbs 6g
Ingredients:
- 1 cup of milk
- 2 sliced onions
- 1 (around 2 pounds) of beef tenderloin
- 3 tablespoons of mayonnaise
- Salt and ground black pepper to taste
- 1 1/2 cups of mature Cheddar cheese grated

Instructions:
- Preheat your air fryer at 400°F. Cooking spray a casserole dish large enough to suit your air fryer.
- Thinly slice the beef and pound it into finger-sized pieces with a meat mallet. Layer one at a time. Season with salt and pepper to taste. Place the onion in the dish and top with the cheddar cheese.
- Mayonnaise and milk should be mixed together and evenly poured over the cheese. Fill the air fryer basket halfway with them.
- Cook for approximately 20 to 25 minutes and serve hot.

5. Air Fried Peppercorn-Crusted Beef Tenderloin

Preparation time: 10 minutes
Cooking time: 25 minutes
Servings 6
Nutrition facts (Per serving) Calories 289 Fat 13.8g Protein 34.7g Carbs 1.6g
Ingredients:
- 2 lbs. of beef tenderloin, trimmed and tied
- 2 tablespoons of avocado oil
- 1 teaspoon of coarse salt
- 3 tablespoons of whole green peppercorns (coarsely ground)
- 2 teaspoons of roasted minced garlic

Instructions:
- Inside a small-sized dish, combine the salt, roasted garlic, and oil. Rub it all over the beef tenderloin.
- On a plate, spread the ground peppercorns and coat the tenderloin in them to form a crust. Place them in the air fryer basket.
- Cook for about 25 minutes at 400°F. Turn the tenderloin halfway through cooking.

6. Air Fryer Roasted Beef with Onion Gravy

Preparation time: 10 minutes
Cooking time: 30 minutes
Servings 12
Nutrition facts (Per serving) Calories 281 Fat 18.5g Protein 23.8g Carbs 3.4g
Ingredients:
- 1 (around 3 pounds) of boneless beef eye of round roast
- 1/4 cup of almond flour
- 1 finely chopped small onion
- 3 cloves of minced garlic
- 1 (around 26 ounces) of carton Swanson Beef Stock or Swanson®

- 2 tablespoons of olive oil
- 1/2 teaspoon of ground black pepper
- Beef Stock unsalted
- 1 tablespoon of finely chopped fresh parsley

Instructions:
- Preheat your air fryer at 400°F. To save the fluids, roast the meat in a small-sized pan, fatty side up. Combine half of the pepper with the beef.
- In the air fryer, cook for around 30 minutes. Remove the meat from the pan and set aside for 25 minutes before cutting.
- Heat the oil inside the roasting pan over medium flame. To the pan, add the garlic, onion, remaining black pepper, and parsley. Continue to stir and heat till soft, scraping the browned bits from the pan's bottom. Inside a large-sized mixing bowl, combine the flour and stock till smooth. Fill the pan halfway with the stock mixture. Cook, stirring constantly, till the sauce thickens slightly. Enjoy the meat with the gravy!

7. Air Fried Spicy Beef Strips with Peas

Preparation time: 10 minutes
Cooking time: 15 minutes
Servings 4
Nutrition facts (Per serving) Calories 295 Fat 13.0g Protein 33.7g Carbs 9.8g
Ingredients:
- 2 tablespoons of olive oil
- 1 medium sliced white onion
- 1 pound of sirloin beef, thin strips
- 1 thinly sliced diagonally red hot pepper
- 2 cloves of minced garlic
- 1 medium thinly sliced carrot
- Kosher salt and ground black pepper
- 1 cup of frozen green peas, thawed

Instructions:
- Preheat your air fryer at 400°F.
- Warm the olive oil in a skillet or wok over medium flame. Cook the garlic and onion for 3 to 4 minutes.
- Cook for 5 to 6 minutes or till the meat strips are browned.
- Cook for 5 minutes more after adding the green peas, carrot, and hot pepper. Sprinkle with pepper and salt, and place the mixture in a baking dish that will easily fit your air fryer.
- Cook for approximately 10 to 15 minutes in the air fryer.

8. Air Fried Chipotle Steaks

Preparation time: 10 minutes
Cooking time: 20 minutes
Servings 4
Nutrition facts (Per serving) Calories 283 Fat 19.2g Protein 24.2g Carbs 1.8g
Ingredients:
- 6 oz. of plain Greek yogurt
- 1/2 teaspoon of the ground cumin
- Kosher salt, to taste
- 1/4 cup of chopped cilantro
- 4 beef sirloin
- 1 chipotle chili in adobo sauce
- 1/4 teaspoon of dried dill

Instructions:
- Preheat your air fryer at 400°F.
- Combine the yogurt, cilantro, chipotle, dill, and cumin.
- Add the chipotle sauce mixture to a ziplock bag and season with salt.
- Toss the beef in the marinade to coat both sides. Refrigerate the bag for approximately 2 hours.
- Place the beef in the air fryer basket.
- Cook for about 15 to 20 minutes, turning halfway.

9. Air Fried Steak with Chimichurri

Preparation time: 10 minutes
Cooking time: 20 minutes
Servings 8
Nutrition facts (3 ounces cooked steak with 3 tablespoons sauce) Calories 336 Fat 26g Protein 22g Carbs 4g

Ingredients:
- 5 sliced garlic cloves
- 1/4 cup of white wine vinegar
- 1 to 2 chipotle peppers in adobo sauce
- 1/4 cup of lime juice
- 2 cups of fresh parsley leaves
- 1-1/2 cups of cilantro leave fresh
- 1/2 cup of olive oil
- 3/4 teaspoon of pepper, divided
- 1/2 coarsely chopped medium red onion
- 2 pounds of beef flat iron steaks or 2 beef top sirloin steaks (1 pound each)
- 1 teaspoon of lime zest grated
- 1-1/4 teaspoons of salt, divided
- 3 teaspoons of dried oregano

Instructions:
- Preheat your air fryer at 390°F.
- Inside a food processor, combine parsley, cilantro, red onion, chipotle peppers, and garlic cloves; process until completely chopped; then add oil, lime zest, vinegar, lime juice, 1/2 teaspoon salt, oregano, and 1/4 teaspoon pepper; process till well blended. Transfer to a bowl, cover, and chill.
- Season the steaks with the remaining pepper and salt, then place them in the air fryer basket and cook for around 12 to 15 minutes, flipping halfway through.
- Allow it cool for a few minutes before slicing and serving it with the prepared chimichurri.

10. Air Fried Korean Style Rib Barbecue

Preparation time: 10 minutes
Cooking time: 20 minutes
Servings 5
Nutrition facts (Per serving) Calories 339 Fat 13.0g Protein 39.9g Carbs 12.3g
Ingredients:
- 1/4 cup of soy sauce
- 1/2 teaspoon of ground ginger
- 1/4 cup of rice vinegar
- 1/2 teaspoon 0f garlic powder
- 1/4 cup of water
- 1 teaspoon of hot chili paste
- 1/2 teaspoon of onion powder
- 1 1/2 pounds of beef short ribs trimmed
- 1/2 teaspoon of sesame oil
- 1/4 cup of sugar substitute
- Cooking oil spray

Instructions:
- Preheat your air fryer at 400°F.
- Inside a saucepan, combine soy sauce, water, sugar replacement, and rice vinegar and bring to the boil over high flame. Then reduce the flame to low and continue to cook for about 5 minutes. Remove from the flame and stir in the sesame oil and spices.
- Place the ribs in a container with a lid and coat with marinade on all sides. Close the lid and place it in the refrigerator for 8 hours.
- Place the ribs in a baking dish large enough to accommodate your air basket. Cook for around 15 to 20 minutes.

11. Air Fried Maple Mustard Beef Steaks

Preparation time: 10 minutes
Cooking time: 20 minutes
Servings 4
Nutrition facts (Per serving) Calories 252 Fat 7g Protein 35g Carbs 10g
Ingredients:
- 1/2 teaspoon of cayenne pepper
- 2 tablespoons of sugar-free maple syrup
- 4 of beef tenderloin steak
- 2 tablespoons of Dijon mustard
- 1 teaspoon of garlic powder
- 2 tablespoons of apple cider vinegar
- 1/4 teaspoon of salt

Instructions:
- Preheat your air fryer at 400°F.
- Inside a large-sized mixing bowl, combine maple syrup, Dijon mustard, apple cider vinegar, cayenne pepper, garlic powder, and salt, then add meat and marinate for about 1 hour.

- Cook the steaks in the air fryer basket for about 15 to 20 minutes.

12. Air Fryer Grilled Flank Steaks with Chili

Preparation time: 10 minutes
Cooking time: 20 minutes
Servings 8
Nutrition facts (Per serving) Calories 253 Fat 13.3g Protein 30.5g Carbs 1.0g
Ingredients:
- 1 lb. of flank steak
- 2 tablespoons of olive oil
- 1 teaspoon of onion powder
- 1/2 teaspoon of the ground cumin
- 1/4 cup of apple cider vinegar
- 1 tablespoon of red hot chili pepper
- Salt and freshly ground black pepper
- 1 teaspoon of minced garlic

Instructions:
- Preheat your air fryer at 400°F.
- Put all of the ingredients in a zip lock bag, then add the flank steak and toss to cover all sides. Refrigerate for approximately 2 hours.
- Remove from the refrigerator after 2 hours and discard the marinade.
- Cook for around 15 to 20 minutes in the air fryer, turning halfway through.

13. Air Fried Seared Beef Ribeye

Preparation time: 10 minutes
Cooking time: 45 minutes
Servings 2
Nutrition facts
(Per serving) Calories 377 Fat 30.7g Protein 22.6g Carbs 0.4g
Ingredients:
- 1/4 teaspoon of pepper
- 1 tablespoon of fresh thyme
- 1/4 teaspoon of garlic powder
- 2 Ribeye Steaks medium
- 1/2 teaspoon of dried oregano
- 1 tablespoon of avocado oil
- 1/2 teaspoon of salt
- 1/4 cup of butter at room temperature
- 1/4 teaspoon of dried parsley

Instructions:
- Rub the steak with pepper and salt before placing it in the air fryer basket.
- Cook for about 45 minutes at 250°F.
- Warm the avocado oil over medium heat, then sear both sides of the steak until the oil is hot. Remove from the pan once done.
- In a small cup, combine butter, garlic powder, parsley, thyme, and oregano.
- Top the steak with the prepared herb butter.

14. Air Fried Beef Yakitori

Preparation time: 10 minutes
Cooking time: 20 minutes
Servings 4
Nutrition facts (Per serving) Calories 392 Fat 19g Protein 37g Carbs 20g
Ingredients:
- 1 pound of beef sirloin, thin long strips
- 2 tablespoons of lemon juice
- 2 finely chopped green onions
- 1 teaspoon of sesame seeds
- 2 tablespoons of sugar substitute
- 1/3 cup of soy sauce
- 2 tablespoons of vegetable oil
- 1/2 teaspoon of minced fresh ginger
- 2 cloves of minced garlic

Instructions:
- Preheat your air fryer at 400°F.
- Combine all of the ingredients inside a medium-sized dish.
- Arrange the steak on skewers in a sewing pattern, pressing the wooden skewer in and out of the beef.
- To properly coat them, dip them in the marinade. Refrigerate the skewers for about 1 hour.
- Place the skewers in an air fryer basket and cook for 15 to 20 minutes, flipping once halfway through.

15. Air Fried Beef Bulgur Patties

Preparation time: 10 minutes
Cooking time: 15 minutes
Servings 8
Nutrition facts (Per serving) Calories 230 Fat 6.6g Protein 29.7g Carbs 12.4g
Ingredients:
- 1 cup of cooked bulgur
- 3/4 cup of whole-wheat breadcrumbs
- 1.5 lbs. of ground beef
- 1/4 cup of cilantro
- 1 clove of garlic
- 1/2 cup of onion chopped
- 1 egg whole
- Fresh ground black pepper
- 1 package of ranch dressing mix

Instructions:
- Preheat your air fryer at 400°F.
- Inside a medium-sized mixing bowl, combine all of the ingredients and shape them into 8 burger patties.
- Cook the patties in the air fryer basket for about 15 minutes.

16. Air Fried Garlic Butter Flavored Steak Bites

Preparation time: 5 minutes
Cooking time: 15 minutes
Servings 4
Nutrition facts (Per serving) Calories 313 Fat 17g Protein 37g Carbs 1g
Ingredients:
- 1 tablespoon of parsley
- Salt & pepper or steak spice, to taste
- 1 1/2 pounds of sirloin steak or strip loin or ribeye
- 1 teaspoon of fresh rosemary or 1/2 teaspoon of dried rosemary
- 2 tablespoons of butter
- 1 tablespoon of vegetable oil or as needed
- 2 cloves of minced garlic

Instructions:
- Preheat your air fryer at 390°F.
- Cut the steak into bite-size pieces. Combine with the pepper, salt, and rosemary.
- Place them in the air fryer basket and brush them with 1 tablespoon of vegetable oil. Cook for 10 to 15 minutes, flipping halfway through.
- Cook garlic and butter in a pan for about 1 minute or until fragrant. Toss in steak and parsley to coat.
- Remove from flame and serve immediately!

17. Air Fried Mini Meatloaf Muffins

Preparation time: 10 minutes
Cooking time: 20 minutes
Servings 10 muffins
Nutrition facts (Per serving) Calories 227 Fat 11g Protein 15g Carbs 15g
Ingredients:
- 1 1/2 pounds of lean ground beef
- 2 tablespoons of parsley
- 1/2 finely diced onion
- 3/4 cup of seasoned bread crumbs
- 1/2 finely diced green pepper
- 1 tablespoon of Worcestershire sauce
- 1/4 cup of barbecue sauce
- 1 egg
- Salt and pepper to taste

For the Glaze:
- 1/3 cup of chili sauce
- 1 tablespoon of sugar substitute
- 1/3 cup of ketchup

Instructions:
- Preheat the air fryer at 390°F. Set aside 10 ramekins after coating them.
- Set aside the glaze ingredients after mixing.
- On medium flame, sauté onion in 1 tablespoon of oil for 5 minutes or till tender. Allow it to totally cool.
- Combine all ingredients, including 1/4 cup of glaze mixture. Mix them till completely combined.
- Divide the mixture among 10 ramekins and top each with 1 tablespoon of the glaze mixture.

- Cook for around 15 to 20 minutes.

18. Air Fried Soy Ginger Beef Skewers

Preparation time: 10 minutes
Cooking time: 15 minutes
Servings 4 skewers
Nutrition facts (Per serving) Calories 232 Fat 8g Protein 27g Carbs 10g
Ingredients:
- 1 clove of minced garlic
- 2 green thinly sliced onions
- 1 pound of cubed sirloin steak (or your favorite cut of beef)
- 1 tablespoon of vegetable oil
- 1/2 cup of low sodium soy sauce
- 1 tablespoon of sugar-free maple syrup
- 2 tablespoons of lemon juice
- 1 onion sliced into large pieces
- 1/2 tablespoon of fresh ginger minced or grated

Instructions:
- Preheat your air fryer at 390°F.
- Combine the vegetable oil, soy sauce, maple syrup, green onions, garlic, lemon juice, and ginger in a zip-lock bag.
- Place the steak cubes in the marinade and leave for 4 to 6 hours.
- Thread one slice of onion and one piece of meat onto skewers.
- Cook for about 15 minutes, flipping the skewers halfway.

19. Air Fried Beef Tagliata

Preparation time: 20 minutes
Cooking time: 20 minutes
Servings 6
Nutrition facts (Per serving) Calories 333 Fat 18.5g Protein 45.5g Carbs 3g
Ingredients:
- 3 large minced cloves of garlic
- 2 teaspoons of ground black pepper, divided
- 6 cups of loosely packed arugula
- 2 teaspoons of fresh rosemary finely chopped
- 1 teaspoon of fresh oregano chopped
- 1/4 sliced lemon
- 2 teaspoons of extra virgin olive oil
- 1 tablespoon of sea salt, divided
- 2 ounces of Parmesan cheese, shaved
- 1 tablespoon of extra-virgin olive oil
- 2 (1 1/2) pounds of sirloin steaks, around 1 1/2-inches thick
- 1 teaspoon of lemon juice

Instructions:
- Preheat your air fryer at 390°F.
- Inside a small-sized bowl, combine the rosemary, oregano, garlic, and 1 1/2 teaspoons of salt. Brush the steaks with the spice mixture.
- Place the steak in the skillet with 1 tablespoon of olive oil. Switch to the air fryer basket. Cook for about 20 minutes or till both sides of the steaks are browned.
- Transfer the steak to a cutting board and set aside for 10 minutes before slicing. Spread arugula on a dish and top with steak slices. Lemon juice, 2 teaspoons olive oil, and parmesan cheese on top.

20. Air Fried Beef Patties Smothered in Mushrooms Sauce

Preparation time: 10 minutes
Cooking time: 15 minutes
Servings 4
Nutrition facts (Per serving) Calories 365 Fat 22.3g Protein 23.6g Carbs 15.8g
Ingredients:
- 1 tablespoon of Worcestershire sauce
- 1 (10.75 ounces) can of Campbell's Condensed Cream of Mushroom Soup (Regular or 98% Fat-Free)
- 1 finely chopped small onion
- 1 1/2 cups of mushrooms sliced
- 1 pound of ground beef
- 1/3 cup of Italian-seasoned dry bread crumbs
- 1 beaten egg

- 2 tablespoons of water
- 1 tablespoon of vegetable oil

Instructions:
- Preheat your air fryer at 390°F.
- Inside a large-sized mixing bowl, combine the beef, bread crumbs, 1/4 cup soup, egg, and onion. Form the beef mixture into four patties.
- Cook for around 10 to 15 minutes in the air fryer. Halfway through, flip them over.
- In a pan, heat 1 tablespoon of oil and add the remaining soup and water. Bring the Worcestershire sauce and mushrooms to a boil. Cook for about 5 minutes on low flame after adding the prepared patties.

21. Air Fried Beef Tenderloin with Garlic Mushroom Sauce

Preparation time: 15 minutes
Cooking time: 20 minutes
Servings 4
Nutrition facts (Per serving) Calories 394 Fat 23.6g Protein 35.2g Carbs 6.7g
Ingredients:
- 2 cups of baby portabella mushrooms sliced
- 4 (7 ounces) of beef tenderloin steaks (around 1 1/2 inches thick)
- 2 tablespoons of beef broth
- 1 (9 ounces) pouch of creamy portabella mushroom cooking sauce
- 3 tablespoons of butter
- 4 finely chopped cloves of garlic

Instructions:
- Heat up your air fryer at 390°F.
- Put steaks in the air fryer basket and rub them with pepper, salt, and 1 tablespoon of butter. Cook for about 15 to 20 minutes.
- In a pan, put 2 tablespoons of butter, garlic, and mushrooms. Cook for about 4 to 5 minutes, then add the beef broth and cooking sauce. Turn down the flame and let it simmer for 4 to 5 minutes. Keep stirring.
- Steaks taste great with mushroom sauce on top.

22. Air Fried Beef and Egg Bake

Preparation time: 10 minutes
Cooking time: 20 minutes
Servings 12
Nutrition facts (Per serving) Calories 218 Fat 11g Protein 20g Carbs 9g
Ingredients:
- 4 cups of frozen hash brown potatoes shredded
- 1 pound of ground beef
- 1/2 teaspoon of red pepper flakes
- 14 eggs large
- 1 1/3 cups of halved tomatoes
- 2 teaspoons of onion powder
- 1 1/2 teaspoons of salt
- 1 teaspoon of pepper
- 10 ounces of chopped frozen spinach
- 3/4 cup of Monterey Jack cheese shredded
- 1 teaspoon of garlic powder
- 1/2 teaspoon of rubbed sage
- 1 cup of ricotta cheese
- 1/3 cup of milk

Instructions:
- Heat up your air fryer at 400°F.
- Cook the beef, onion powder, salt, garlic powder, sage, and pepper flakes inside a large-sized skillet for around 6 to 8 minutes, or till the beef changes color and falls apart. Drain. Mix the spinach in well. Turn off the flame of the pan.
- Mix all the ingredients in a greased baking dish. Spread the beef mixture out evenly on top of the potatoes. Whisk together the eggs, ricotta cheese, milk, pepper, and the rest of the salt inside a large-sized bowl. Pour the mixture on top of the cheese and sprinkle with more cheese. Make a layer of tomatoes on top of that.
- Cook for around 20 minutes in the air fryer.

23. Air Fried Steak Pinwheels

Preparation time: 10 minutes
Cooking time: 20 minutes
Servings 8

Nutrition facts (2 pinwheels) Calories 224 Fat 12g Protein 26g Carbs 1g
Ingredients:
- 2 (1 pound each) of beef flank steaks, trimmed
- 1 cup of green onions finely chopped
- 1/2 pound of cooked and crumbled bacon strips
- 2 tablespoons of minced chives
- 1/4 cup of finely chopped fresh basil or 4 teaspoons dried basil
- 1 cup of finely chopped fresh mushrooms

Instructions:
- Heat up your air fryer at 400°F.
- Flatten steaks till they are 1/4 inch thick. Mix the bacon, onions, mushrooms, basil, and chives together in a big bowl, then spread the mixture over the steaks evenly.
- Roll the meat up and use toothpicks or skewers to hold it together. Use a toothpick to secure each roll into pieces that are 1/2 to 3/4 inches long. Put them in the air fryer basket and let them cook for about 15 to 20 minutes. Take the toothpicks out before you eat.

24. Air Fried Italian-Style Meatloaf

Preparation time: 10 minutes
Cooking time: 20 minutes
Servings 8
Nutrition facts (Per serving) Calories 261 Fat 14g Protein 25g Carbs 10g
Ingredients:
- 1/2 cup of red onion chopped
- 1 cup of marinara or spaghetti sauce
- 1/2 cup of old-fashioned oats
- 1 large lightly beaten egg
- 1/2 teaspoon of pepper
- Parmesan cheese shredded, optional
- 1/4 cup of ground flaxseed
- 1 pound of lean ground beef (90% lean)
- 1/4 pound of chopped fresh mushrooms
- 1 package (19-1/2 ounces) of Italian turkey sausage links, casings removed, crumbled

Instructions:
- Heat up your air fryer at 390°F.
- Inside a large bowl, mix the oats, egg, mushrooms, onion, pepper, and flax. Crumble the turkey and beef over the mixture and stir it slowly but thoroughly.
- Use your hands to shape the mixture into a loaf shape, then put it in a greased baking dish that will fit in your air fryer.
- After about 15 minutes, put marinara sauce on top and bake for another 5 minutes. Slice before serving.

25. Air Fried Thai-Style Beef Tri-Tip

Preparation time: 10 minutes
Cooking time: 30 minutes
Servings 8
Nutrition facts (Per serving) Calories 362 Fat 15.5g Protein 39.4g Carbs 14.9g
Ingredients:
- 2 tablespoons grated onion
- 3 tablespoons of soy sauce
- 6 crushed cloves of garlic
- 1/3 cup of lemongrass chopped
- 2 teaspoons of ground turmeric
- 1/3 cup of fish sauce
- 3 tablespoons of fresh ginger root grated
- 1 tablespoon of ground cumin
- 1/4 cup of seasoned rice vinegar
- 2 tablespoons of ground coriander
- 1/2 teaspoon of cayenne pepper
- 2 tablespoons of olive oil
- 1 (2 1/2 pounds) of trimmed beef tri-tip roast
- 1/3 cup of sugar substitute

Instructions:
- Heat up your air fryer at 400°F.
- Inside a large-sized bowl, mix together the garlic, lemongrass, grated onion, grated ginger root, rice vinegar, fish sauce, soy sauce, coriander, cumin, cayenne pepper, turmeric, sugar substitute, and olive oil. Whisk till all of the ingredients are mixed well.
- Put the tri-tip roast all the way into the marinade. Poke the roast with the tines of

a fork several times on both sides to get the marinade inside. Use plastic wrap to cover the dish. Refrigerate for 2 to 12 hours. During the marinating time, take the meat out of the fridge every now and then to turn it and poke it with a fork.

- For a few minutes, let the roast drain on a tray lined with paper towels. Put the sauce aside.
- Cook in the air fryer for about 25 to 30 minutes, basting halfway through with the marinade and turning once.
- In a saucepan, bring to a boil any extra marinade. For 1 to 2 minutes, cook. This sauce could be used to serve the food.

26. Air Fryer Corned Beef Brisket

Preparation time: 15 minutes
Cooking time: 35 minutes
Servings 6
Nutrition facts (Per serving) Calories 455 Fat 33.7g Protein 30.6g Carbs 5.4g
Ingredients:

- 1 tablespoon of vegetable oil
- 2 tablespoons of water
- 1 sliced onion
- 1 (5 pounds) of corned beef brisket flat-cut
- 6 cloves of sliced garlic
- 1 tablespoon of browning sauce

Instructions:

- Heat up your air fryer at 390°F.
- Take any seasoning packets out of the corned beef and throw them away. Browning sauce should be used on both sides of the brisket. In a wide skillet over medium-high flame, heat the oil and brown the brisket on both sides, which should take about 5 to 8 minutes.
- Put the brisket in a pan to roast. Sprinkle onion and garlic slices over the brisket and add water to the roasting pan. Wrapped foil around the pan in a tight way.
- Cook in the air fryer for about 30 to 35 minutes.

27. Air Fried Asian-Style Beef Skewers

Preparation time: 10 minutes
Cooking time: 20 minutes
Servings 6
Nutrition facts (Per serving) Calories 136 Fat 4.9g Protein 14.7g Carbs 6.7g
Ingredients:

- 1 tablespoon of minced fresh ginger root
- 1 1/2 pounds of flank steak
- 2 chopped green onions
- 3 tablespoons of hoisin sauce
- 2 cloves of minced garlic
- 1/4 cup of soy sauce
- 3 tablespoons of grape vinegar
- 1 teaspoon of barbeque sauce
- Skewers

Instructions:

- Heat up your air fryer at 390°F.
- Inside a small-sized dish, mix together hoisin sauce, grape vinegar, soy sauce, barbecue sauce, garlic, green onions, and ginger.
- Cut the flank steak across the grain into 1/4-inch slices. Fill a 1-gallon bag that can be closed with slices halfway. Pour the mixture of hoisin sauce and water over the slices and toss to mix. Put it in the fridge for at least two hours or overnight.
- Take the steaks out of the marinade and put them on the skewer.
- Cook for about 15 to 20 minutes, turning the meat over once halfway through.

28. Air Fried Barbarian Beef

Preparation time: 10 minutes
Cooking time: 20 minutes
Servings 8 (1 2 1/2-pound steak)
Nutrition facts (Per serving) Calories 243 Fat 13g Protein 28.6g Carbs 0.9g
Ingredients:

- 1 (around 2 1/2 pounds) of boneless top round steak, or to taste
- Salt, according to taste

For the Sauce:

- 2 tablespoons of red wine vinegar
- 4 cloves of garlic
- 1 Fresno chili pepper
- 2 teaspoons of rosemary leaves
- 1 teaspoon of kosher salt
- 2 tablespoons of olive oil

Instructions:
- Season both sides of the beef with salt. Let sit at room temperature for about 30 minutes.
- Put the beef in the basket of the air fryer and cook it at 370°F for 15 to 20 minutes. Halfway through cooking, turn the food over.
- Put the chili pepper, rosemary, garlic, and kosher salt in a mortar and grind them together. Crush into a paste with a pestle. Mix in the oil and vinegar.
- Before cutting, spread sauce on top.

29. Air Fried Sesame Beef

Preparation time: 10 minutes
Cooking time: 15 minutes
Servings 4
Nutrition facts (Per serving) Calories 354 Fat 22.5g Protein 22.2g Carbs 15.8g
Ingredients:
- 2 chopped green onions
- 4 tablespoons of olive oil
- 2 minced cloves of garlic
- 4 tablespoons of soy sauce
- 1 pound of round steak
- 4 tablespoons of sugar substitute
- 2 tablespoons of sesame seeds

Instructions:
- Heat up your air fryer at 400°F.
- Mix the soy sauce, oil, sugar substitute, garlic, and onions inside a large-sized bowl. Put them away.
- Slice the steak into strips and put them in the dish. Cover and put in the fridge for at least half an hour.
- Put them in the basket of the air fryer and cook for about 15 to 20 minutes or till they are done. When you serve it, sprinkle more sesame seeds on top.

30. Air Fried Greek-Style Meatballs

Preparation time: 10 minutes
Cooking time: 20 minutes
Servings 5
Nutrition facts (Per serving) Calories 265 Fat 19g Protein 18g Carbs 5g
Ingredients:
- 1/3 cup of panko bread crumbs
- 3 tablespoons of chopped fresh mint
- 1/2 teaspoon of cumin
- 2 tablespoons of milk
- 1/2 pound of pork or ground lamb
- 1 teaspoon of lemon zest
- 1/2 teaspoon of dried oregano
- 2 tablespoons of chopped parsley
- 1/2 pound of lean ground beef
- 1 egg
- 1/4 cup of finely chopped red onion
- 2 cloves of minced garlic
- 1/2 teaspoon of salt

Instructions:
- Heat up your air fryer at 400°F.
- Panko bread crumbs and milk should be mixed together and left to sit for about 5 minutes.
- Mix the rest of the ingredients together till they are well blended. Use the mixture to make 20 balls.
- Put the balls in the basket of the air fryer and bake for about 20 minutes or till they are done.

Chapter 8: Poultry Recipes

1. Air-Fried Butter Parmesan Chicken

Preparation time: 10 minutes
Cooking time: 25 minutes
Servings 6
Nutrition facts (Per serving) Calories 391 Fat 24g Protein 33g Carbs 10g
Ingredients:
- 1/2 cup of Dijon mustard
- 2 cups of bread crumbs soft
- 6 skinless and boneless chicken breast halves (6 ounces each)
- 1 cup of parmesan cheese grated
- 1/2 cup of melted butter

Instructions:
- Heat up your air fryer at 380°F.
- Inside a large-sized bowl, mix together the bread crumbs, cheese, and butter. Spread mustard all over the chicken, and then roll it in the bread crumbs. Move them to the basket of the air fryer and spray them with cooking spray.
- Cook for about 15 to 20 minutes, turning over halfway.

2. Air-Fried Onion Chicken

Preparation time: 10 minutes
Cooking time: 20 minutes
Servings 4
Nutrition facts (Per serving) Calories 460 Fat 36g Protein 23g Carbs 10g
Ingredients:
- 1 teaspoon of ground mustard
- 4 skinless and boneless chicken breast halves (4 ounces each)
- 1 (2.8 ounces) can of crushed French-fried onions
- 1/2 cup of melted butter
- 1 tablespoon of Worcestershire sauce

Instructions:
- Heat up your air fryer at 350°F.
- Mix Worcestershire sauce, butter, and mustard inside a medium-sized bowl. Keep the onions in a separate dish that's about the same size. To finish, dip the chicken breast in the butter mixture and spread thin slices of onion over it.
- Place the chicken in a greased baking dish. Pour the rest of the butter mixture on top of the chicken. Move to the basket of the air fryer.
- Air fry for about 20 minutes.

3. Air Fried Delicious Chicken Gratin

Preparation time: 10 minutes
Cooking time: 15 minutes
Servings 6
Nutrition facts (For 6 people serving: 1 1/3 cups) Calories 709 Fat 54g Protein 34g Carbs 19g
Ingredients:
- 3 cups of refrigerated and cooked spinach tortellini
- 2 cans of artichoke hearts water-packed (14 ounces each)
- 1 1/2 cups of Asiago cheese grated, divided
- 3 cups of cooked and shredded chicken
- 1 1/2 cups of mayonnaise

Instructions:
- Heat up your air fryer at 350°F.
- Save 1/4 cup of the juice from the artichokes and throw away the rest. Finely chop and mix with tortellini, 1 cup of cheese, mayonnaise, chicken, and 1/4 cup of the reserved artichoke juice in a mixing dish.
- Pour the artichoke mixture into a baking dish that has been greased, and then sprinkle the rest of the cheese on top. Transfer to air fryer basket.
- Cook for about 15 minutes or till the top is bubbling and lightly browned.

4. Air Fried Herbed Turkey Meatballs

Preparation time: 10 minutes
Cooking time: 20 minutes
Servings 5
Nutrition facts (Per serving) Calories 214 Fat 9.4g Protein 19.1g Carbs 13.2g
Ingredients:
- 1 lb. of lean ground turkey breast
- 1/4 cup of chopped onion
- 1 egg whole
- 1/4 cup of grated parmesan cheese
- 1 tablespoon of chopped fresh rosemary
- Olive oil spray
- 1 tablespoon of chopped fresh parsley leaves
- 1/2 cup of breadcrumbs
- 1 teaspoon of minced garlic
- Kosher salt and pepper, to taste

Instructions:
- Heat up your air fryer at 390°F.
- Mix all of the ingredients together inside a bowl. Mix everything well.
- About 2 tablespoons of the beef mixture should be used to make small balls.
- Put the meatballs in the Air Fryer's cooking basket. Spray with oil and cook for about 15 minutes or till golden brown.
- Put on a platter to serve. If you think it needs it, add more chopped parsley and Parmesan cheese on top.

5. Air-Fried Polynesian Kebabs

Preparation time: 5 minutes
Cooking time: 20 minutes
Servings 14 kebabs
Nutrition facts (Per serving) Calories 95 Fat 6g Protein 5g Carbs 7g
Ingredients:
- 1 package (14 ounces) of breakfast turkey sausage links, cut in half
- 2 tablespoons of sugar-free maple syrup
- 1 can (8 ounces) of whole water chestnuts, drained
- 1/8 teaspoon of ground nutmeg
- 1 can (8 ounces) of unsweetened pineapple chunks
- 2 teaspoons of reduced-sodium soy sauce
- Dash of pepper
- 1 sweet red pepper large, cut into 1-inch chunks

Instructions:
Heat up your air fryer at 400°F.
- After you drain the pineapple, save 1 tablespoon of the pineapple juice (discard the remaining juice or save it for another use). Put the sausages, water chestnuts, red pepper, and pineapple on skewers that have been soaked in water.
- Inside a small-sized cup, mix the maple syrup, soy sauce, pepper, nutmeg, and pineapple juice that you saved.

- About 15 minutes is all it takes to cook kebabs in an air fryer. Halfway through cooking, turn the meat over and baste it with the marinade.

6. Air-Fried Stuffed Turkey Tenderloins

Preparation time: 10 minutes
Cooking time: 30 minutes
Servings 4
Nutrition facts (Per serving) Calories 228 Fat 3g Protein 41g Carbs 14g
Ingredients:
- 2 tablespoons of almond flour
- 1 package (20 ounces) of turkey breast tenderloins
- 1/4 cup of panko bread crumbs
- 1 package (8 ounces) of artichoke hearts frozen, thawed, and chopped
- 2 tablespoons of lemon juice
- 1/2 pound of chopped baby Portobello mushrooms
- 2 1/2 cups of reduced-sodium chicken broth, divided
- 1/2 teaspoon of salt
- 1 teaspoon of lemon zest grated
- 1/4 teaspoon of pepper

Instructions:
- Heat up your air fryer at 390°F.
- Bring mushrooms, artichoke hearts, 1/2 cup broth, and lemon juice to a boil inside a large-sized saucepan. Reduce the flame to low and cook, uncovered, for 7–9 minutes, or till the mushrooms are soft and the liquid is gone. Add the bread crumbs and set the pan aside to cool down a bit.
- Cut each tenderloin in half horizontally through the middle, stopping 1/4 inch from the other edge. Open flat. Use a sharp knife to cut off the white tendons. Cover and use a meat mallet to beat to an even thickness. Take off the lid and dot the tops with the artichoke mixture. Start rolling jelly-roll style from one of the long sides and tie with kitchen string every 3 inches.
- Place the dumplings, seam side down, 1 inch apart in a baking dish, and pour 1 cup of broth on top. Add salt and pepper to the turkey. Put the food in the air fryer.
- Air fry for about 20 minutes.
- Take the turkey out of the pan, cover it with aluminum foil, and let it sit for 5 minutes. In the meantime, mix the rest of the broth with the flour inside a small-sized saucepan till smooth. Then add the juices from the pan. Bring to the boil, then cook and stir for 2–3 minutes or till the sauce has thickened. Take off the string and cut the tenderloins into pieces. Pour gravy on top and sprinkle with lemon zest.

7. Air Fried Filipino Adobo Chicken

Preparation time: 10 minutes
Cooking time: 35 minutes
Servings 8
Nutrition facts (Per serving) Calories 581 Fat 35.4g Protein 58.5g Carbs 3g
Ingredients:
- 6 pounds of bone-in chicken thighs skin-on
- 1/2 cup of soy sauce
- 4 bay leaves
- 1 cup of distilled white vinegar
- 12 smashed and peeled cloves of garlic
- 2 teaspoons of black peppercorns whole

Instructions:
- Heat up your air fryer at 380°F.
- Inside the bottom of a baking dish that fits easily in your air fryer, layer the chicken thighs, bay leaves, peppercorns, garlic, soy sauce, and vinegar. Make sure the peppercorns and bay leaves are covered in the liquid. Move the dish around in the basket of the air fryer.
- Cook in the air fryer for around 30 to 35 minutes.

8. Air Fried Chicken Stuffed with Mozzarella and Asparagus

Preparation time: 10 minutes

Cooking time: 25 minutes
Servings 2
Nutrition facts (Per serving) Calories 390 Fat 10.8g Protein 57.4g Carbs 13.3g
Ingredients:
- 2 large boneless and skinless chicken breast halves
- 1/2 cup of shredded mozzarella cheese, divided
- 1/4 cup of Italian seasoned bread crumbs
- 8 trimmed asparagus spears, divided
- Salt and black pepper to taste

Instructions:
- Heat up your air fryer at 400°F.
- Each chicken breast should be spread out on a flat, firm surface between two heavy plastic sheets. Use the smooth side of a meat mallet to pound the chicken till it is about 1/4 inch thick and evenly spread out. Sprinkle both sides using salt and pepper.
- Place four asparagus spears down the middle of a chicken breast and cover with about 1/4 cup of mozzarella cheese. Repeat with the other chicken breasts, rolling the chicken around the asparagus and cheese to make a neat roll.
- Cook for about 20 to 25 minutes in the air fryer.

9. Air Fried Spicy Buttermilk Chicken

Preparation time: 10 minutes
Cooking time: 20 minutes
Servings 4
Nutrition facts (Per serving) Calories 298 Fat 7.5g Protein 31g Carbs 27.8g
Ingredients:
- 2 cups of Buffalo wing sauce
- Cooking spray
- 4 boneless and skinless chicken breast halves
- 1 clove of minced garlic
- 1/2 teaspoon of salt
- 2 cups of buttermilk
- 1/4 teaspoon of ground black pepper
- 2 tablespoons of Dijon mustard

Instructions:
- Heat up your air fryer at 390°F.
- Mix the buffalo sauce, the mustard, the buttermilk, the salt, the garlic, and the pepper inside a shallow cup. Stir in the chicken breasts. Marinate in the fridge for 12 to 24 hours with the lid on.
- Place the chicken and marinade in a greased baking dish and move to the air fryer basket.
- Cook for 20 minutes or till there are no more juices in the pan.

10. Air Fried Lemon-Butter Chicken Tenders

Preparation time: 10 minutes
Cooking time: 20 minutes
Servings 8
Nutrition facts (Per serving) Calories 81 Fat 3.3g Protein 11.5g Carbs 0.9g
Ingredients:
- 1/4 teaspoon of paprika
- 1/3 cup of lemon juice
- 8 skinless and boneless chicken tenders
- Cooking spray
- 4 teaspoons of softened butter
- 1/2 teaspoon of salt

Instructions:
- Heat up your air fryer at 390°F. Using cooking spray, grease a baking dish.
- Put chicken tenders in a single layer on a baking dish that has been greased. Spread butter on the tenders, then drizzle lemon juice evenly over them. Add paprika and salt to taste. Place the dish in the basket of the air fryer.
- Cook for about 20 minutes or till the dish no longer has any liquid.

11. Air Fried Asian-Style Chicken Tandoori

Preparation time: 10 minutes
Cooking time: 20 minutes
Servings 6

Nutrition facts (Per serving) Calories 246 Fat 9.2g Protein 35.4g Carbs 3.1g

Ingredients:
- 1/3 cup of tandoori paste
- 1/4 teaspoon of Kosher salt
- 1 white onion medium, cut into rings, to serve
- 1/4 teaspoon of ground black pepper
- 1 teaspoon of ground cumin
- 1/2 cup of plain Greek-style yogurt
- Lettuce leaves, to serve
- 1 1/2 lbs. of chicken breast fillet

Instructions:
- Preheat your air fryer at 400°F.
- Combine the tandoori paste, yogurt, and cumin inside a nonreactive mixing cup; season using salt and pepper. Make a thorough mixture.
- Turn the chicken over to coat both sides with sauce. Cover and chill for at least an hour to ingest all of the spices.
- Place the chicken in a baking dish that fits easily into the Air Fryer basket.
- Cook for 20 minutes, basting using pan juices. On a serving tray, arrange the chicken tandoori with lettuce leaves and onion rings.

12. Air Fried Chicken, Pepper, Bean, Tomato Roast

Preparation time: 10 minutes
Cooking time: 20 minutes
Servings 6
Nutrition facts (Per serving) Calories 274 Fat 12g Protein 34g Carbs 6g

Ingredients:
- 2 tablespoons of olive oil
- 1/4 teaspoon of Kosher salt
- 1 medium chopped onion
- 2 tablespoons of fresh mixed herbs
- 1 medium diced red bell pepper
- 1/2 cup of tomato puree
- 1 1/2 lbs. of diced breast fillet of chicken
- 4 oz. of green beans, cut into small pieces
- 1 tablespoon of minced garlic
- 2 diced tomatoes
- 1/4 teaspoon of freshly ground black pepper

Instructions:
- Preheat your air fryer at 400°F.
- Heat the oil inside a medium-sized pan over medium-high flame. Cook till the garlic and onion are aromatic.
- Cook for around 7 to 8 minutes or till the chicken is golden brown. Add the tomatoes, bell pepper, tomato puree, green beans, and herbs. Cook for 7 minutes more, covered, stirring periodically. Season with salt and pepper to taste.
- Place in an Air Fryer-compatible baking dish. Cook for approximately 15 to 20 minutes.

13. Air Fried Peri-Peri Chicken

Preparation time: 10 minutes
Cooking time: 20 minutes
Servings 8
Nutrition facts (Per serving) Calories 259 Fat 12.9g Protein 30.1g Carbs 2.2g

Ingredients:
- 3 tablespoons of hot paprika
- 3/4 cup of fresh lemon juice
- 4 quarter legs of chicken
- 2 teaspoons of grated fresh ginger
- 3 cloves of minced garlic
- 1/2 teaspoon of kosher salt
- 2 tablespoons of hot chili powder

Instructions:
- Preheat your air fryer at 400°F.
- Combine lemon juice, paprika, chili powder, garlic, ginger, and salt inside a non-reactive cup.
- To coat evenly, toss in the leg quarters. Allow for at least 2 hours of marinating time.
- Place the marinated leg pieces in the air fryer basket. Cook in the air fryer for 20 to 25 minutes or till well fried.

14. Air Fried Whole Roasted Chicken with Vegetables

Preparation time: 10 minutes

Cooking time: 40 minutes
Servings 8
Nutrition facts (Per serving) Calories 260 Fat 11.2g Protein 33.4g Carbs 5.4g
Ingredients:
- 2 tablespoons of lemon juice
- 1/2 teaspoon of cayenne pepper
- 1 tablespoon of sugar-free maple syrup
- 2 tablespoons of olive oil
- 1/2 teaspoon of dried thyme
- 1 stick of celery, cut into 1-inch pieces
- 8 black olives
- Salt and pepper, to taste
- 2 tablespoons of butter melted
- 1 chicken whole
- 2 tablespoons of Dijon mustard
- 1 tablespoon of chopped fresh rosemary
- 2 carrots, cut into sticks
- 1 teaspoon of minced garlic
- 1/2 teaspoon of onion powder

Instructions:
- Preheat your air fryer to 360°F.
- Inside a small-sized bowl, combine the lemon juice, melted butter, mustard, maple syrup, and rosemary. Thoroughly combine. Coat all sides of the chicken.
- Inside a large-sized mixing bowl, combine the cayenne pepper, olive oil, garlic, onion powder, and dried thyme. Toss the vegetables in the dressing to coat. Season using salt and pepper to taste.
- Place the chicken in a baking dish that will fit in the cooking basket of your air fryer. Arrange the vegetables on the plate's sides. In a preheated air fryer, cook for 35 to 40 minutes or till the chicken is cooked through. Serve immediately and enjoy!

15. Air Fried Chicken Yakitori

Preparation time: 10 minutes
Cooking time: 20 minutes
Servings 4
Nutrition facts (Per serving) Calories 276 Fat 9.2g Protein 21.7g Carbs 14.8g
Ingredients:
- 2 tablespoons of sugar substitute
- 1/2 cup of soy sauce
- 10 wooden skewers
- 1 teaspoon of olive oil, or to taste
- 4 scallions, cut into 1-inch pieces
- 3 tablespoons of Japanese rice vinegar
- 4 boneless and skinless chicken thighs, cut into 1-inch cubes
- 1/2 cup of chicken broth

Instructions:
- Preheat your air fryer at 400°F.
- Thread the chicken and scallions alternately onto the wet skewers.
- Bring chicken broth, soy sauce, Japanese rice vinegar, and sugar substitute to a boil inside a small-sized saucepan. Reduce the flame to low and continue to cook for 5 minutes. Set aside half of the sauce for dipping.
- Place the skewers in an air fryer basket, spray using oil, and cook for 15 to 20 minutes, flipping once halfway through the air frying. Baste frequently with half of the sauce.

16. Air Fried Balsamic Chicken

Preparation time: 10 minutes
Cooking time: 20 minutes
Servings 4
Nutrition facts (Per serving) Calories 194 Fat 4.9g Protein 26.4g Carbs 9.8g
Ingredients:
- 4 boneless and skinless chicken breast halves
- 1 minced clove garlic
- 1/3 cup of balsamic vinegar
- 1 tablespoon of olive oil
- 1/2 cup of chicken broth
- 2 tablespoons of sugar substitute
- 1 teaspoon of dried Italian herb seasoning

Instructions:
- Preheat your air fryer at 380°F.
- Combine the balsamic vinegar, chicken broth, sugar replacement, garlic, and Italian seasoning inside a mixing dish; add the chicken breasts and marinate for 10 minutes on each side.

- Drizzle the chicken with olive oil and set aside the marinade in the air fryer basket. Cook for 10 to 15 minutes, flipping halfway through.
- Pour the marinade into a large-sized skillet and simmer till slightly thickened, about 5 minutes, flipping the chicken breasts once or twice.

17. Air Fried Lemon-Oregano Chicken

Preparation time: 10 minutes
Cooking time: 20 minutes
Servings 6
Nutrition facts (Per serving) Calories 277 Fat 6.9g Protein 44.3g Carbs 7.2g
Ingredients:
- 3 cloves of minced garlic
- 2 teaspoons of dried oregano
- 3 pounds of boneless and skinless chicken breast halves
- 2 tablespoons of sugar-free maple syrup
- 3 tablespoons of lemon juice
- 1 tablespoon of olive oil

Instructions:
- Preheat your air fryer at 380°F.
- Place the chicken breast halves in a greased baking dish large enough to accommodate your air fryer. Combine the lemon juice, maple syrup, olive oil, garlic, and oregano inside a mixing bowl. Mixture should be poured over the chicken breasts.
- Cook for around 15 to 20 minutes in the air fryer or till the chicken is no longer pink on the interior, and the juices flow clear.

18. Air Fried Horseradish-Crusted Turkey Tenderloin

Preparation time: 10 minutes
Cooking time: 20 minutes
Servings 4
Nutrition facts (Per serving) Calories 230 Fat 9g Protein 30g Carbs 8g
Ingredients:
- 2 tablespoons of horseradish prepared
- 1 green chopped onion
- 1/2 cup of soft bread crumbs
- 2 tablespoons of reduced-fat mayonnaise
- 1 pound of turkey breast tenderloins
- 2 tablespoons of fresh parsley minced

For the sauce:
- 1/4 cup of reduced-fat mayonnaise
- 1 tablespoon of Dijon mustard
- 1/4 teaspoon of paprika
- 2 tablespoons of fat-free milk
- 1/4 cup of fat-free plain yogurt
- 1 tablespoon of prepared horseradish

Instructions:
- Preheat your air fryer at 400°F.
- Inside a mixing bowl, combine the mayonnaise and horseradish. Inside a small-sized bowl, combine bread crumbs, green onion, and parsley. Spread the mayonnaise mixture over the tenderloins, then coat with the crumb mixture. Place the air fryer basket in the air fryer.
- Cook for around 15 to 20 minutes in the air fryer. In a mixing bowl, combine the sauce ingredients. Serve with the turkey.

19. Air Fried Cajun Chicken

Preparation time: 10 minutes
Cooking time: 20 minutes
Servings 10
Nutrition facts
(Per serving) Calories 536 Fat 47.8g Protein 24.8g Carbs 1.8g
Ingredients:
- 2 cups of olive oil
- 10 boneless and skinless chicken breast halves - pounded to 1/2-inch thickness
- 2 tablespoons of dried Italian-style seasoning
- 2 tablespoons of Cajun seasoning
- Garlic powder to taste
- 2 tablespoons of lemon pepper

Instructions:
- Preheat your air fryer at 390°F.
- Inside a large-sized shallow bowl, combine the Cajun seasoning, oil, Italian seasoning, garlic powder, and lemon pepper. Toss the

chicken around in the dish to properly coat it with the sauce. Refrigerate for 30 minutes after covering.
- Remove the chicken from the marinade and set aside. Cook the chicken in the air fryer for 6 to 8 minutes on each side or till the juices run clear.

20. Air Fried Turkey Saltimbocca

Preparation time: 10 minutes
Cooking time: 20 minutes
Servings 2
Nutrition facts (Per serving) Calories 300 Fat 17g Protein 29g Carbs 4g
Ingredients:
- 1/4 cup of almond flour
- 2 tablespoons of fresh sage minced
- 1/8 teaspoon of pepper
- 1 (8 ounces) turkey breast tenderloin
- 1 1/2 teaspoons of olive oil
- 1 thin slice of prosciutto or deli ham, sliced into thin strips
- 2 tablespoons of melted butter
- 1/4 cup of chicken broth

Instructions:
- Preheat your air fryer at 390°F.
- Sift the flour into a large-sized shallow bowl. Tenderloin should be cut in half horizontally and flattened using a meat mallet to a thickness of 1/2 inch. Season using salt & pepper to taste. Flour both sides and shake off the excess.
- Inside a large-sized skillet over medium heat, melt 1 tablespoon of butter and oil. Cook the turkey for 2 minutes on each side or till no longer pink.
- In the air fryer basket, cook for around 15 to 20 minutes.
- Heat 1 1/2 teaspoons of butter over a medium-high flame in the same pan. Cook, stirring constantly, till the prosciutto is slightly crisped. Increase the heat to medium-high and pour in the chicken broth. Cook, stirring to scrape up browned bits from the bottom of the pan till the liquid is somewhat reduced. Remove the pan from the flame and stir in the remaining 1-1/2 teaspoons of butter. Serve with the turkey

21. Air Fried Nepiev Chicken

Preparation time: 10 minutes
Cooking time: 20 minutes
Servings 4
Nutrition facts (Per serving) Calories 239 Fat 9.6g Protein 28.2g Carbs 9.1g
Ingredients:
- 4 boneless, skinless chicken breast halves – 1/4-inch thickness
- 1 tablespoon of Italian seasoning
- 4 tablespoons of cream cheese spread, garlic flavored
- 1 tablespoon of garlic powder
- 1/4 cup of garlic and herb-seasoned dry bread crumbs
- 1 tablespoon of onion powder
- Salt and pepper to taste
- 1 tablespoon of olive oil
- 1 tablespoon of butter

Instructions:
- Preheat your air fryer at 400°F.
- In a cup or small tub, combine the Italian seasoning, garlic powder, and onion powder. Season both sides of the chicken using salt and pepper. 1 tablespoon cream cheese, slightly spread out in the center of each slice Roll up and tuck the sides in. To keep everything together, use toothpicks.
- Distribute the bread crumbs on a plate or in a shallow dish. Roll the chicken rolls in bread crumbs to coat. Place on a tray, wrap with plastic wrap and place in the freezer for 30 minutes.
- Melt the butter and oil in a medium-sized saucepan over medium-high flame. Browning the chicken rolls on all sides will take about 5 minutes. Fill the air fryer basket halfway with rolls.
- In the air fryer, cook for around 15 minutes.

22. Air Fried Teriyaki Chicken

Preparation time: 10 minutes
Cooking time: 30 minutes
Servings 6
Nutrition facts (Per serving) Calories 232 Fat 5.0g Protein 34.0g Carbs 11.1g
Ingredients:
- 1 1/2 lbs. breast fillet of chicken, cut into strips
- Black pepper to taste
- 1/4 cup of mirin (Japanese sweet rice wine)
- 1 teaspoon of minced fresh ginger
- 2 tablespoons of rice vinegar
- Toasted sesame seeds
- 1/4 cup of soy sauce
- 1 teaspoon of sesame oil
- 3 cloves of minced garlic
- 1/4 cup of sugar substitute

Instructions:
- Preheat your air fryer at 360°F.
- Combine soy sauce, mirin, rice vinegar, sesame oil, sugar replacement, garlic, and ginger inside a small-sized cup.
- Fill a resealable container halfway with the teriyaki sauce mixture. To taste, add a pinch of black pepper.
- Then, add the chicken strips and rub them in the marinade, ensuring they are completely covered on both sides. Refrigerate for at least two hours.
- Remove the marinated chicken from the resealable bag and set it in an Air Fryer-compatible baking dish.
- Cook in the Air Fryer for around 20-25 minutes, stirring halfway through. When ready to serve, toss with toasted sesame seeds.

23. Air Fried Turkey Loaf

Preparation time: 10 minutes
Cooking time: 40 minutes
Servings 6
Nutrition facts (Per serving) Calories 269 Fat 7.0g Protein 31.1g Carbs 19.4g
Ingredients:
- 1 tablespoon of sugar-free maple syrup
- 2 teaspoons of Worcestershire sauce
- 1-1/2 lbs. of ground turkey
- 1 tablespoon of chopped fresh rosemary
- 1/4 cup of catsup
- 1 egg whole
- 1/2 teaspoon of ground coriander
- 1 medium chopped white onion
- 1/4 cup of whole milk
- 2 tablespoons of Dijon mustard
- 1/3 cup of tomato sauce
- 1 tablespoon of chopped fresh thyme
- 3/4 cup of whole-wheat breadcrumbs
- Kosher salt and ground black pepper

Instructions:
- Preheat your air fryer at 330°F.
- Inside a large-sized mixing bowl, combine the ground turkey and the remaining ingredients (excluding the catsup). Mix everything together with your hands till everything is well blended. Season using salt and pepper to taste.
- Place the turkey mixture in an Air Fryer-compatible baking dish or loaf pan. Catsup should be applied to the tip.
- Cook for approximately 30 to 40 minutes in the Air Fryer. Allow to cool slightly before serving.

24. Air Fried Buttery Maple Chicken

Preparation time: 10 minutes
Cooking time: 15 minutes
Servings 4
Nutrition facts (Per serving) Calories 235 Fat 8.8g Protein 29.1g Carbs 8.9g
Ingredients:
- 2 tablespoons of sugar-free maple syrup
- 1 teaspoon of minced garlic
- 1/4 teaspoon of salt
- 4 breast fillets of chicken
- 2 tablespoons of butter
- 1/2 teaspoon of ground coriander

Instructions:
- Preheat your air fryer at 400°F.
- Combine the maple syrup, butter, coriander, garlic, and salt inside a large non-reactive mixing dish. After fully mixing, add

the chicken fillets. Allow at least one hour for marinating.
- Cook the chicken fillets for around 15 to 20 minutes in the Air Fryer grill pan or till done to your liking.

25. Air Fried Spicy Barbecue Chicken

Preparation time: 10 minutes
Cooking time: 15 minutes
Servings 4
Nutrition facts (Per serving) Calories 234 Fat 10.2g Protein 29.1g Carbs 6.4g
Ingredients:
- 1/2 teaspoon of kosher salt
- 2 tablespoons of olive oil
- 1/2 teaspoon of ground coriander
- 4 breast fillet of chicken
- 1/2 teaspoon of ground black pepper
- 1 teaspoon of minced garlic
- 1/4 cup of barbecue sauce
- 1 teaspoon of paprika

Instructions:
- Preheat your air fryer at 400°F.
- Combine the olive oil, barbecue sauce, garlic, paprika, coriander, salt, and pepper in a large non-reactive mixing bowl. After fully mixing, add the chicken fillets. Allow at least two hours for marinating.
- Cook for about 15 minutes or till the marinated chicken fillets are well cooked.

26. Air Fried Chicken Tikka

Preparation time: 10 minutes
Cooking time: 25 minutes
Servings 8
Nutrition facts (Per serving) Calories 205 Fat 5.6g Protein 31.0g Carbs 2.5g
Ingredients:
- 1 teaspoon of paprika
- 1/2 cup of plain Greek yogurt
- 1 tablespoon of crushed garlic
- 1 tablespoon of olive oil
- 2.2 lbs. of chicken tenders, each sliced in half
- 1 teaspoon of Garam Masala
- 2 teaspoons of lemon juice
- 1 teaspoon of cayenne pepper
- 1/4 cup of chopped fresh parsley, chopped
- 1 teaspoon of salt
- Cooking oil spray
- 1 tablespoon of grated ginger
- Chopped fresh cilantro for garnish
- 1 teaspoon of turmeric

Instructions:
- Preheat your air fryer at 400°F.
- Inside a non-reactive dish, combine the chicken, parsley, yogurt, ginger, garlic, salt, cayenne pepper, garam masala, turmeric, paprika, olive oil, and lemon juice. Thoroughly combine. After covering, refrigerate for at least 2 hours.
- Place the marinated chicken chunks in the air fryer basket. Cook for around 20 to 25 minutes, flipping halfway through.
- Place in a serving dish and decorate with cilantro.

27. Air Fried Drumsticks with Thyme Mustard Sauce

Preparation time: 5 minutes
Cooking time: 30 minutes
Servings 8
Nutrition facts (Per serving) Calories 259 Fat 12.7g Protein 32.4g Carbs 2.2g
Ingredients:
- 2 tablespoons of chopped fresh thyme
- 3 cloves of minced garlic
- 2 tablespoons of Dijon mustard
- Salt and freshly ground black pepper
- 1 1/2 lbs. of chicken drumsticks
- 1 cup of sour cream
- 2 teaspoons of wholegrain mustard

Instructions:
- Preheat your air fryer at 380°F.
- Combine the Dijon, sour cream, whole grain mustard, thyme, and garlic inside a small-sized bowl. Thoroughly combine.

Fill a large-sized baking dish to fit within your Air Fryer basket with the ingredients.
- Toss in the drumsticks and turn to evenly coat. Season using salt and pepper to taste.
- Cook for 25 to 30 minutes in the air fryer or till thoroughly cooked, rotating halfway through. Garnish with a sprig of thyme if preferred.

28. Air Fried Garlic-Mustard Chicken

Preparation time: 10 minutes
Cooking time: 25 minutes
Servings 6
Nutrition facts (Per serving) Calories 255 Fat 11.9g Protein 33.8g Carbs 1.6g
Ingredients:
- 1 1/2 lbs. of breast fillet of chicken
- 2 tablespoons of Dijon mustard
- 1/4 teaspoon of ground black pepper
- 1 tablespoon of minced garlic
- 1/2 cup of sour cream
- Steamed vegetables, to serve
- 2 teaspoons of wholegrain mustard
- 1/4 teaspoon of Kosher salt

Instructions:
- Preheat your air fryer at 380°F.
- Combine the wholegrain mustard, garlic, Dijon mustard, and sour cream inside a medium-sized mixing bowl. Thoroughly combine. Fill a baking dish with the mixture that will easily fit in your Air Fryer basket.
- Toss in the chicken and turn to evenly coat. Season using salt and pepper to taste.
- Cook for around 20 to 25 minutes, stirring occasionally, or till the chicken is cooked through.
- Serve with cooked mixed vegetables on the side.

29. Air Fried Chicken Breast with Veggies

Preparation time: 10 minutes
Cooking time: 40 minutes
Servings 5
Nutrition facts (Per serving) Calories 276 Fat 12.2g Protein 25.1g Carbs 17.4g
Ingredients:
- 10 of marbled potatoes, washed thoroughly (optional)
- 1/2 teaspoon of dried rosemary
- 2 cups of broccoli florets
- 1 carrot medium, sliced into sticks
- 4 chicken breasts, boneless and skinless
- 2 tablespoons of lemon juice
- 1 tablespoon of sugar-free maple syrup
- 2 tablespoons of olive oil
- 1/2 teaspoon of dried basil
- 1 tablespoon of Dijon mustard
- 1/2 teaspoon of cayenne pepper
- 1 teaspoon of minced garlic
- 1/2 teaspoon of garlic powder
- Salt and pepper, to taste

Instructions:
- Preheat your air fryer at 360°F.
- Inside a small-sized bowl, place the chicken breast. Combine the mustard, maple syrup, garlic powder, rosemary, and cayenne pepper. To coat, thoroughly combine all ingredients.
- Inside a mixing bowl, combine the olive oil, lemon juice, basil, and garlic. Toss the vegetables in the dressing to coat. Add salt and pepper to taste.
- In the Air Fryer cooking basket, cook vegetables for about 20 minutes or till the potatoes are soft. Place the vegetables on a platter and cover them with foil to keep them warm.
- Cook the marinated chicken breasts in the same Air Fryer cooking basket for around 20 minutes or till cooked through.
- Place the chicken on a dish and serve with the roasted veggies on the side.

30. Air Fried Chicken Meatballs

Preparation time: 10 minutes
Cooking time: 20 minutes
Servings 6
Nutrition facts (Per serving) Calories 269

Fat 14g   Protein 25g Carbs 8g

Ingredients:
- 3/4 cup of dry bread crumbs
- 2 lightly beaten whole eggs
- 1/4 cup of cream cheese
- 1/2 tablespoon of garlic powder
- 1 teaspoon of ground cumin
- 1/2 teaspoon of ground black pepper
- 1 lb. of ground chicken
- Fresh parsley
- 1/2 teaspoon of Kosher salt
- Cooking oil spray

Instructions:
- Preheat your air fryer at 400°F.
- Combine the ground chicken, beaten eggs, cream cheese, bread crumbs, cumin, garlic powder, salt, and pepper inside a large-sized mixing bowl. Thoroughly combine.
- Form 1 tablespoon of the chicken mixture into little meatballs. Arrange them in an Air Fryer basket. Coat in oil.
- Cook for approximately 15–20 minutes or till golden brown.
- Transfer to a serving plate and serve. As a finishing touch, sprinkle with chopped parsley.

Chapter 9: Pork Recipes

1. Air-Fried Pork Chops Stuffed with Mushroom Sauce

Preparation time: 10 minutes
Cooking time: 20 minutes
Servings 4
Nutrition facts (Per serving) Calories 326 Fat 14g Protein 31g Carbs 15g
Ingredients:
- 6 oz. box stuffing mix, any flavor of your choice, or 2 cups homemade stuffing
- 10.5 oz. of cream of mushroom soup
- 4 boneless pork chops, thick-cut, about 1 inch
- Salt & black pepper to taste

Instructions:
- Preheat your air fryer at 370°F.
- Make the stuffing mix according to the package directions. Allow it to totally cool.
- Season the pork chops using salt and pepper to taste. To construct a pocket for the stuffing, butterfly the pork open with a knife.
- Fill a casserole dish with 1/3 cup of filling for each pork chop. Combine any remaining stuffing with the pork in the pan.
- Season each pork chop with pepper and serve with condensed mushroom soup on the side.
- Cook for around 20 minutes in the air fryer.

2. Air-Fried Balsamic Pork Loin

Preparation time: 10 minutes
Cooking time: 35 minutes
Servings 8
Nutrition facts (Per serving) Calories 398 Fat 16g Protein 51g Carbs 7g
Ingredients:
- 3 1/2-4 pounds of pork loin

For the Marinade:
- 1 teaspoon of kosher salt
- 4 minced garlic cloves
- 1/2 cup of white wine vinegar
- 2 tablespoons of sugar-free maple syrup
- 1 teaspoon of black pepper
- 2 teaspoons of fresh thyme leaves
- 1/4 cup of olive oil
- 2 teaspoons of chopped fresh rosemary
- 1/4 cup of balsamic vinegar

Instructions:
- Preheat your air fryer at 390°F.
- Inside a medium-sized mixing bowl, combine the marinade ingredients.
- Pour the marinade mixture over the pork loin inside a large zip-top bag. Allow at least 3 hours or overnight marinating time.
- Place the marinated pork loin in a casserole dish.
- Cook for around 40 minutes in the air fryer, basting the pork every 10 minutes.

3. Air-Fried Pork Tenderloin with Dijon Sauce

Preparation time: 10 minutes
Cooking time: 30 minutes
Servings 4

Nutrition facts (Per serving) Calories 387 Fat 31g Protein 25g Carbs 2g

Ingredients:
- 1 tablespoon of Dijon mustard
- 2 tablespoons of olive oil, divided
- 1 pound of pork tenderloin
- Kosher salt and black pepper to taste

For the Creamy Dijon Sauce:
- 1/2 teaspoon of dry mustard powder
- 3/4 cup of chicken broth
- 1 tablespoon of Dijon mustard
- 1 clove of minced garlic
- 3/4 cup of heavy cream
- 1 tablespoon of butter
- 1/2 teaspoon of dried thyme

Instructions:
- Preheat your air fryer at 390°F.
- Combine Dijon mustard and 1 tablespoon olive oil inside a small-sized cup. After spraying the pork tenderloin with oil, season it with pepper and salt.
- Heat 1 tablespoon of olive oil in a large-sized skillet over medium-high flame. Brown the pork on all sides for about 2-3 minutes per side, then transfer it to the air fryer basket. Cook for around 18 to 20 minutes.
- While the pork is cooking, melt the butter with the garlic in the same pan and sauté for 1 minute or till the garlic is fragrant. Add chicken broth after scraping up any brown pieces with the back of a spoon.
- Inside a mixing bowl, combine the Dijon mustard, cream, mustard powder, and thyme. Bring to the boil, then reduce to a low flame and cook until the sauce thickens about 8-10 minutes. Take the pan off the flame.
- Remove the pork from the air fryer and set it aside to rest for 5 minutes. Serve with a side of mustard sauce.

4. Air-Fried Sheet Pan Pork with Asparagus

Preparation time: 10 minutes
Cooking time: 20 minutes
Servings 4
Nutrition facts (Per serving) Calories 486 Fat 23g Protein 37g Carbs 32g

Ingredients:
- 3 cups of cut fresh asparagus (1-inch pieces)
- 2 teaspoons of sugar substitute
- 4 pork loin chops boneless (1-inch-thick and around 6 ounces each)
- 1/4 cup of olive oil, divided
- 2 teaspoons of Southwest seasoning
- 1/4 teaspoon of pepper
- 3 cups of diced new potatoes or any other veggie of your choice
- 1 teaspoon of ground cinnamon
- 1/4 teaspoon salt
- 1 large peeled gala or Honey crisp apple, 1-inch wedges
- 1/4 teaspoon of ground ginger

Instructions:
- Preheat your air fryer at 390°F.
- Line a baking pan that fits comfortably inside your air fryer with foil and spray with 2 tablespoons of olive oil.
- Inside a large-sized mixing bowl, toss potatoes with 1 tablespoon of olive oil. Place in one of the prepared baking pan sections. In the same dish, toss asparagus with 1 tablespoon of olive oil and place in a different portion of the plate. Season the asparagus and potatoes using salt and pepper.
- In the same dish, toss the apple with 1 teaspoon of olive oil. In a small-sized dish, combine sugar substitute, cinnamon, and ginger; sprinkle over apples and toss to coat. Transfer to a different section of the pan.
- Brush the pork chops with the remaining 1 tablespoon of olive oil and season both sides with Southwest seasoning. Place the chops in the remaining pan space.
- Cook for around 15 to 20 minutes in the air fryer.

5. Air Fried Orange Spiced Ham Steak

Preparation time: 10 minutes
Cooking time: 20 minutes
Servings 4
Nutrition facts (2 ounces of cooked ham) Calories 188 Fat 8g Protein 14g Carbs 16g
Ingredients:
- 1 bone-in ham steak (about 1 pound)
- 2 tablespoons of water
- 1 teaspoon of corn syrup
- 1/8 to 1/4 teaspoon of ground ginger
- 1 tablespoon of prepared mustard
- 1/4 cup of orange marmalade
- 1 tablespoon of butter

Instructions:
- Preheat your air fryer at 380°F.
- Place the ham in the air fryer basket and cook for around 15 minutes.
- Inside a medium-sized skillet, bring the remaining ingredients to a boil. Cook, covered, for about 1-2 minutes or till the ham is cooked through.

6. Air Fried Pork Tenderloin Stuffed with Pepper

Preparation time: 10 minutes
Cooking time: 25 minutes
Servings 8
Nutrition facts (3 slices) Calories 201 Fat 8g Protein 26g Carbs 5g
Ingredients:
- 3 pork tenderloins (around 3/4 pound each)
- 2 finely chopped small celery ribs
- 3/4 teaspoon of paprika
- 4 teaspoons of lemon-pepper seasoning
- 2 tablespoons of olive oil
- 3 finely chopped small sweet red peppers
- 1 1/2 teaspoons of dried thyme
- 4 teaspoons of crushed fennel seed
- 3/4 teaspoon of garlic salt
- 1 finely chopped large onion
- 1/2 teaspoon of cayenne pepper

Instructions:
- Preheat your air fryer at 400°F.
- Inside a large-sized skillet over medium-high flame, heat the oil. Cook for 3-4 minutes or till red peppers, onion, and celery are soft. Cook for 1 minute more after adding the thyme, garlic salt, paprika, and cayenne. Set the pan aside after removing it from the flame.
- Make a slit through the center of each tenderloin, stopping approximately 1/2 inch from the rim. Tenderloins should be lying flat and open. Using a meat mallet, flatten the pork to a thickness of 1/2 inch. Fill with a vegetable and stuffing mixture. Tenderloins should be tied at 2-inch intervals with kitchen string, with the ends sealed with toothpicks.
- Place on a frying spray-coated air fryer basket. Tenderloins should be rubbed using a mixture of lemon pepper and fennel.
- Cook for around 25 minutes in the air fryer, flipping halfway through. Before serving, cut into 8 pieces and remove toothpicks and threads.

7. Air-Fried Sautéed Pork Chops with Garlic Spinach

Preparation time: 5 minutes
Cooking time: 25 minutes
Servings 4
Nutrition facts (1 pork chop with 1/2 cup of spinach) Calories 310 Fat 17g Protein 36g Carbs 4g
Ingredients:
- 1 tablespoon of olive oil
- 1/4 teaspoon of salt
- 4 (8 ounces each) bone-in pork loin chops
- 1/4 teaspoon of pepper
- 1 lemon medium

For the garlic spinach:
- 1/2 teaspoon of salt
- 1 tablespoon of olive oil
- 1/4 teaspoon of coarsely ground pepper
- 2 packages (5 ounces each) of fresh spinach, stems removed
- 1 teaspoon of lemon juice

- 3 thinly sliced garlic cloves

Instructions:
- Preheat your air fryer at 400°F.
- Season the pork chops using salt and pepper, then coat them with oil and place them in the air fryer.
- Cook for around 20 minutes in the air fryer. Place the chops on a serving plate and drizzle with lemon juice. Wrap in foil and place and set it aside for at least 5 minutes before serving.
- For the garlic spinach, heat the oil over a medium-high flame. Cook, stirring regularly, for 45 seconds or till the garlic begins to color. Cook, occasionally stirring, till the spinach is wilted, about 2-3 minutes. Season with salt and pepper to taste. Remove from the flame and stir in the lemon juice. Place on a plate to serve. Remove the foil from the pork chops and serve with spinach.

8. Air-Fried Orange-Glazed Pork Loin

Preparation time: 10 minutes
Cooking time: 30 minutes
Servings 16
Nutrition facts (4 ounces cooked pork with 1 tablespoon of glaze) Calories 199 Fat 7g Protein 28g Carbs 6g
Ingredients:
- 1 minced garlic clove
- 1/4 teaspoon of ground ginger
- 1 teaspoon of salt
- 1/4 teaspoon of pepper
- 1 (5 pounds) of boneless pork loin roast
- 3 fresh thyme sprigs

For the glaze:
- 1 cup of orange juice
- 1 tablespoon of Dijon mustard
- 1/4 cup of packed sugar substitute
- 1 tablespoon of cornstarch
- 1/3 cup of cold water

Instructions:
- Preheat your air fryer at 390°F.
- Combine the salt, garlic, fresh thyme, ground ginger, and pepper inside a mixing bowl. The mixture should be rubbed all over the roast. Place the fat side up in a shallow roasting dish and transfer it to the air fryer basket.
- Cook for around 20 to 25 minutes in the air fryer.
- Meanwhile, in a saucepan over medium flame, combine the orange juice, sugar replacement, and mustard. Inside a small-sized dish, whisk together the water and cornstarch till smooth. Mix in the orange juice mixture. Bring to the boil, then reduce to a low flame for 2 minutes, stirring occasionally. Set aside 1 cup of the glaze for serving; brush half of the remaining glaze over the roast.
- Cook for 10 minutes more, brushing with the leftover glaze as needed. Allow for a 10-minute rest before slicing. Serve the roast with the reserved glaze.

9. Air-Fried Maple-Glazed Pork Chops

Preparation time: 5 minutes
Cooking time: 20 minutes
Servings 4
Nutrition facts (1 pork chop) Calories 316 Fat 13g Protein 33g Carbs 15g
Ingredients:
- 2 teaspoons of Worcestershire sauce
- 1 tablespoon of Dijon mustard
- 4 pork loin chops boneless (1-inch-thick and 6 ounces each)
- 1/4 cup of sugar-free maple syrup
- 1/2 cup of brewed coffee
- 1 teaspoon of minced fresh thyme
- 1/2 teaspoon of pepper
- 1 tablespoon of olive oil
- 1/2 teaspoon of salt

Instructions:
- Preheat your air fryer at 400°F.
- Season the pork chops using thyme, salt, and pepper before placing them in the air fryer basket. Drizzle some oil on top.

- Cook for around 15 minutes in the air fryer.
- In the skillet, combine the remaining ingredients. Bring to the boil, then reduce to a simmer till the liquid is reduced by half.
- In the skillet, place the pork chops. Reduce the heat to low, cover, and simmer for 5 minutes, turning once, until the meat is cooked. Serve with extra sauce on the side.

10. Air-Fried Pork Stuffed with Cheese, Spinach and Pesto

Preparation time: 10 minutes
Cooking time: 20 minutes
Servings 4
Nutrition facts (Per serving) Calories 402 Fat 25g Protein 37g Carbs 4g
Ingredients:

- 1 cup of fresh baby spinach
- 1/4 teaspoon of pepper
- 10 bacon of strips
- 1 cup of shredded Italian cheese blend
- 1/3 cup of prepared pesto
- 1 (1 pound) pork tenderloin

Instructions:

- Preheat your air fryer at 400°F.
- Arrange bacon pieces lengthwise, overlapping slightly
- Tenderloin should be cut lengthwise across the center and to within 1/2 inch of the rim. Open tenderloin flat and pound with a meat mallet to 1/2-inch thickness. Place the tenderloin perpendicular to the bacon strips in the center. Season the pork using salt and pepper. Layer pesto on the bottom, followed by cheese and spinach on top. Overlap the ends of the bacon to cover the tenderloin. Tie with kitchen cord at 3-inch intervals. With toothpicks, secure the ends.
- Cook for around 20 minutes in the air fryer basket, flipping halfway through.

11. Air-Fried Pork Medallions with Balsamic Raspberry Sauce

Preparation time: 5 minutes
Cooking time: 25 minutes
Servings 4
Nutrition facts
(3 ounces cooked pork with 2 tablespoons of sauce) Calories 271 Fat 7g Protein 23g Carbs 28g
Ingredients:

- 2 teaspoons of Dijon mustard
- 1 (1 pound) pork tenderloin, cut into 1-inch slices
- 1 tablespoon of olive oil
- 2 tablespoons of balsamic vinegar
- 1 teaspoon of garlic powder
- 1/2 cup of seedless raspberry puree

Instructions:

- Preheat your air fryer at 400°F.
- Flatten pork to 1/2-inch thickness, season using garlic powder, coat with oil, and place in an air frying basket.
- Cook for about 20 minutes in the air fryer, flipping halfway through.
- Inside a medium-sized saucepan, combine the raspberry puree, vinegar, and mustard. Cook, stirring regularly, for around 2-3 minutes or till the sauce has thickened. Serve with the pork.

12. Air-Fried Pork Chops with Beans

Preparation time: 10 minutes
Cooking time: 40 minutes
Servings 4
Nutrition facts (Per serving) Calories 297 Fat 5g Protein 19g Carbs 45g
Ingredients:

- 2 minced garlic cloves
- 1 3/4 cups of lima beans frozen, thawed
- 4 pork loin chops (around 1/2 inch thick)
- 1 1/2 teaspoons of sugar substitute
- 1 can (16 ounces) of kidney beans, drained and rinsed
- 1/4 teaspoon of salt
- 2 medium chopped onions
- 1 teaspoon of prepared mustard
- 1/4 teaspoon of pepper
- 1 tablespoon of olive oil

- 1/4 cup of chili sauce

Instructions:
- Preheat your air fryer at 370°F.
- Season the pork chops using salt and pepper. Inside a large-sized skillet over medium-high heat, heat the oil. The chops should be cooked on both sides. Transfer to the casserole dish. Remove all except 1 tablespoon of the skillet drippings. Add the onion and cook, stirring regularly, until soft. Cook for 1 minute, stirring regularly, after adding the garlic. Combine the chili sauce, sugar replacement, and mustard in a mixing bowl. Distribute the sauce over the chops.
- Place the dish in an air fryer basket and cook for 20 minutes; after 20 minutes, add the beans and cook for another 20 minutes.

13. Air-Fried Plum-Glazed Pork Kebabs

Preparation time: 5 minutes
Cooking time: 20 minutes
Servings 6
Nutrition facts (1 kebab) Calories 196 Fat 4g Protein 24g Carbs 15g
Ingredients:
- 2 (3/4 pound each) pork tenderloins
- 1 green pepper medium
- 1 minced garlic clove
- 2 tablespoons of reduced-sodium soy sauce
- 1/2 teaspoon of ground ginger
- 1/3 cup of plum jam
- 1 red onion small
- 1 medium sweet red pepper

Instructions:
- Preheat your air fryer at 400°F.
- Inside a small-sized bowl, combine the jam, soy sauce, garlic, and ginger to form the glaze. Cut vegetables and pork into 1-inch slices. Thread alternately pork and veggies onto six metal or moistened wooden skewers. Coat the air fryer basket using cooking oil spray before placing it in the air fryer.
- Cook for around 15 minutes in the air fryer, flipping halfway through and brushing with 1/4 cup glaze during the last 5 minutes. Brush with the leftover glaze before serving.

14. Air-Fried Southwestern-Style Pineapple Pork Chops

Preparation time: 10 minutes
Cooking time: 30 minutes
Servings 4
Nutrition facts (1 pork chop with 1/3 cup of sauce) Calories 274 Fat 12g Protein 27g Carbs 13g
Ingredients:
- 4 pork loin chops boneless (5 ounces each)
- 1 tablespoon of olive oil
- Fresh cilantro minced
- 1 cup of medium salsa
- 1/2 teaspoon of garlic pepper blend
- 1 can (8 ounces) of unsweetened crushed pineapple, undrained

Instructions:
- Preheat your air fryer at 400°F.
- Season the pork chops using pepper and oil. Cook for approximately 10 to 15 minutes on each side in the air fryer basket.

15. Air-Fried Balsamic Glazed Pork and Fig Skewers

Preparation time: 10 minutes
Cooking time: 20 minutes
Servings 12 skewers
Nutrition facts (1 skewer) Calories 139 Fat 4g Protein 13g Carbs 13g
Ingredients:
- 4 thinly sliced fresh basil leaves
- 1 teaspoon of onion powder
- 2 pork tenderloins (around 3/4 pound each), trimmed and silver skin removed
- 1 tablespoon of smoked paprika
- 1/4 teaspoon of cayenne pepper
- 3 tablespoons of sugar-free maple syrup
- 1 teaspoon of salt
- 2 teaspoons of olive oil
- 1/2 cup of blue cheese crumbled

- 12 halved dried figs
- 1/2 teaspoon of white pepper
- 1 teaspoon of pepper
- 1/4 cup of balsamic vinegar
- 12 cherry tomatoes
- 1/2 teaspoon of garlic powder
- 1 tablespoon of Dijon mustard

Instructions:
- Preheat your air fryer at 400°F.
- Pork should be cut into 1-inch chunks. Rub the smoked paprika, pepper, salt, onion powder, garlic powder, white pepper, and cayenne pepper over the meat. Refrigerate and sealed, till ready to cook. Meanwhile, make a glaze with the vinegar, maple syrup, mustard, and oil. Set it aside for now.
- String pork chunks and fig halves onto wooden skewers soaked in water. Cook for 8 minutes on each side in the air fryer. Throughout the second half of the cooking time, brush cooked surfaces using glaze on a frequent basis.
- Allow the skewers to rest for 5 minutes before adding a tomato to each. Serve with a thin coating of blue cheese and basil on a serving dish.
- In an oiled skillet, combine the pineapple and salsa. Bring to the boil. Place the chops in the pan. Reduce the flame to low, cover, and leave to cook for 5 minutes. Garnish with cilantro, if desired.

16. Air-Fried Pork Chop Casserole

Preparation time: 10 minutes
Cooking time: 35 minutes
Servings 4
Nutrition facts (Per serving) Calories 259 Fat 17.7g Protein 12.9g Carbs 12g
Ingredients:
- 1 packet of dry onion soup mix
- 1 (10.75 ounces) can of condensed cream of mushroom soup
- 4 pork chops
- 1 (10.75 ounces) can of water
- 2 tablespoons of olive oil
- 1 cup of diced mushrooms

Instructions:
- Preheat your air fryer at 390°F.
- Inside a medium-sized mixing bowl, combine the onion soup mix, mushroom soup, water, and mushrooms.
- Inside a large-sized skillet set over medium-high flame, brown the pork chops on all sides. In a baking dish, top the chops with the mushroom soup mixture. Place in the air fryer basket.
- Cook for around 30 to 35 minutes in the air fryer.

17. Air-Fried Barbecued Pork Skewers

Preparation time: 5 minutes
Cooking time: 25 minutes
Servings 4
Nutrition facts (Per serving) Calories 359 Fat 21.5g Protein 23.4g Carbs 16.9g
Ingredients:
- 1 (2 pounds) of pork shoulder
- 1/4 cup of grated onion
- 1 finely grated large garlic clove
- 1/2 teaspoon of ground cumin
- 1/2 cup of prepared barbecue sauce
- 1 teaspoon of paprika
- 1/4 teaspoon of cayenne pepper
- 1 tablespoon of sugar substitute
- 2 teaspoons of kosher salt
- 1 teaspoon of ground black pepper

Instructions:
- Preheat your air fryer at 400°F.
- Cut the hog shoulder in half lengthwise with a sharp knife. Each piece should be cut into 1/8-inch thin slices around the grain.
- Inside a mixing bowl, combine the pork, garlic, onion, sugar substitute, cumin, salt, paprika, pepper, and cayenne. Mix it all together with your hands till it's completely smooth.
- Wrap in plastic wrap and chill for at least 4 hours or overnight.

- Thread the pig slices onto skewers, folding the longer portions in half as you go. When assembling the skewer, ensure that the slices are securely packed together.
- Brush on the barbecue sauce and cook for about 10 minutes on each side in the air fryer. Brush with the sauce again 5 minutes before the cooking time is up.

18. Air-Fried Delicious Pork Medallions with Strawberry-Garlic Sauce

Preparation time: 10 minutes
Cooking time: 20 minutes
Servings 4
Nutrition facts (Per serving) Calories 422 Fat 25g Protein 29g Carbs 21g
Ingredients:
- 2 cups of fresh strawberries whole
- 2/3 cup of seasoned bread crumbs
- 2 lightly beaten eggs
- 1/4 cup of water
- 6 tablespoons of butter, divided
- 1/4 teaspoon of salt
- 1 teaspoon of chicken bouillon granules
- 1/2 cup of almond flour
- 1 teaspoon of minced garlic
- Sliced strawberries, optional
- 1 pork tenderloin (around 1 pound)
- 1/4 teaspoon of pepper

Instructions:
- Preheat your air fryer at 400°F.
- Combine water, entire strawberries, and bouillon inside a food processor; process till smooth. Separate the flour, eggs, and bread crumbs into shallow cups.
- Pork should be sliced into 1/2-inch slices and pounded to a thickness of 1/4-inch with a meat mallet. Season with salt and pepper to taste. Flour all sides of the pork and shake off excess. Dip the crumbs into the beaten eggs, then into the crumbs again, patting them down to adhere. Drizzle with 2 tablespoons of melted butter and place in the air fryer basket.
- Cook for around 15 minutes in the air fryer. Turn the medallions halfway through the air frying.
- Sauté the garlic in the remaining butter in the pan. After tossing in the strawberry mixture, heat thoroughly. Serve the pork with the sauce and, if wanted, top it with sliced strawberries.

19. Air-Fried Orange and Curried Pork Kebabs

Preparation time: 5 minutes
Cooking time: 25 minutes
Servings 4
Nutrition facts (1 kebab) Calories 515 Fat 34g Protein 36g Carbs 16g
Ingredients:
- 1 large navel orange unpeeled
- 2 tablespoons of dried minced onion
- 1 sweet yellow or orange pepper large
- 1 1/2 pounds of pork tenderloin
- 1 onion small
- 1/2 cup of olive oil
- 1 minced garlic clove
- 1/2 teaspoon of each ground cumin, cinnamon, and coriander
- 1 to 2 tablespoons of curry powder
- 1 sweet red pepper large

Instructions:
- Preheat your air fryer at 375°F.
- Inside a small-sized bowl, combine the oil, minced onion, garlic, and spices; set aside half of the mixture for basting the kabobs while they cook. Pork, peppers, tomato, and unpeeled orange should be cut into 1-inch chunks. Thread pork, vegetables, and orange on four metal or soaked wooden skewers in alternate directions; brush with the remaining curry mixture.
- Cook for about 10 minutes on each side in the air fryer. During the cooking process, baste with the reserved curry mixture.

20. Air-Fried One-Pan Pork and Squash

Preparation time: 5 minutes
Cooking time: 30 minutes
Servings 4
Nutrition facts (Per serving) Calories 358 Fat 13g Protein 20.3g Carbs 44.5g

Ingredients:

- 5 cups (1-inch) cubes of peeled, seeded butternut squash
- 2 teaspoons of dried sage, divided
- 1 pork tenderloin
- 2 apples, cut into 1-inch wedges
- 3 tablespoons of olive oil, divided
- 2 teaspoons of salt, divided
- 1 white onion, cut into 1/2-inch slices
- Cooking spray
- 2 tablespoons of maple syrup sugar-free
- 1 teaspoon of ground black pepper, divided

Instructions:

- Preheat your air fryer at 400°F.
- Grease a rimmed baking dish large enough to fit your air fryer using cooking oil.
- Whisk together 1 tablespoon of olive oil, 1 teaspoon of salt, maple syrup, 1 teaspoon of sage, and 1/2 teaspoon of pepper inside a mixing dish.
- Place the tenderloin on a baking sheet lined with parchment paper and brush with the mixture.
- Toss the butternut squash, onion, and apples in a large-sized mixing dish with the remaining 2 tablespoons olive oil, 1 teaspoon salt, 1 teaspoon sage, and 1/2 teaspoon pepper. Wrap the pork tenderloin with all of the ingredients.
- Cook in the air fryer for 25 to 30 minutes, or till the veggies are soft and the pork is done, baste the pork several times during cooking with the prepared mixture.

Chapter 10: Dessert Recipes

1. Air-Fried Sugar-free Peanut Butter Cookies

Preparation time: 15 minutes
Cooking time: 10 minutes
Servings 27
Nutrition facts (Per serving) Calories 94 Fat 7g Protein 4g Carbs 3g
Ingredients:
- 1 teaspoon of vanilla extract
- 3/4 cup of peanuts (measured whole, chopped later on)
- 2 Eggs large
- 1/3 cup of stevia
- 1 1/4 cups of peanut butter
- 1/4 teaspoon of sea salt

Instructions:
- Preheat your air fryer at 350°F. Line an air fryer basket using parchment paper.
- Combine the peanut butter, stevia, vanilla, egg, and salt inside a food processor. Scrape down the sides of the mixing bowl as required till the mixture is smooth.
- Pulse in the peanut pieces till uniformly distributed. (Avoid overmixing; you want some crunch.)
- Using a medium cookie scoop, place dough balls 2 inches apart on a prepared air fryer basket. Firmly push the cookie dough into the scoop before releasing it onto the air fryer basket. Flatten with a fork in a crisscross pattern. Between cookies, dip the fork in a cup of cold water and wipe it down with a paper towel. (This will save you from getting stuck.)
- Cook for 5 to 6 minutes in the air fryer or till the cookies are crispy. Transfer to an oven rack or plate to cool before serving.

2. Air-Fried Magic Cookie Bars

Preparation time: 10 minutes
Cooking time: 12 minutes
Servings 16
Nutrition facts (Per serving) Calories 276 Fat 25g Protein 3.5g Carbs 13.5g
Ingredients:
- 1/2 teaspoon of vanilla essence
- 2/3 cup of chopped pecans
- 1 cup of condensed milk sugar-free
- 1/3 cup of shredded coconut unsweetened
- 1 cup of blanched almond flour
- 1/4 cup of stevia
- 1 cup of hazelnut spread sugar-free
- 3 tablespoons of melted butter
- 1/3 cup of dark chocolate chips sugar-free

Instructions:
- Preheat your air fryer at 350°F. Line a sheet pan using parchment paper.
- Inside a medium-sized mixing bowl, combine the almond flour and sweetener.
- Inside a small-sized mixing cup, combine the melted butter and vanilla essence. Press into the almond flour mixture with the back of a spoon or spatula till a crumbly dough forms.
- Firmly push the cookie batter onto the prepared baking sheet.

- Dollop the chocolate hazelnut spread evenly over the crust. First, spread the pecans, next the coconut, and finally, the chocolate chips.
- Pour the condensed milk evenly over the top.
- Cook for around 10 to 12 minutes in the air fryer. Allow the bars to cool completely before removing them from the pan and slicing.

3. Air-Fried Sugar-Free and Low-Carb Banana Bread

Preparation time: 5 minutes
Cooking time: 20 minutes
Servings 8
Nutrition facts (Per serving) Calories 205 Fat 17.2g Protein 8g Carbs 6.4g
Ingredients:
- 1/4 cup of crushed walnuts
- 2 tablespoons of melted butter
- 2 teaspoons of cinnamon
- 1/2 cup of mashed banana, very ripe
- 3 large eggs
- 1/4 cup of granulated erythritol
- 1 teaspoon of baking powder
- 1 1/2 cups of almond flour

Instructions:
- Preheat your air fryer at 350°F.
- Blend in the mashed banana. In an electric mixer, combine the eggs and melted butter and beat till smooth.
- In a separate cup, combine the dry ingredients - baking powder, almond flour, erythritol or other sweetener, and cinnamon. In a medium-sized mixing bowl, whisk together the egg/butter/banana mixture until well combined. Finally, whisk in the crushed walnuts, reserving a few for topping the bread.
- Fill a small lined loaf pan halfway using batter. Cover with the remaining walnuts.
- Cook for around 15 to 20 minutes in the air fryer. Check on the cake after 15 minutes. If the top is already brown, loosely wrap it with aluminum foil to prevent it from burning.

4. Air-Fried Chewy Avocado Brownies

Preparation time: 10 minutes
Cooking time: 15 minutes
Servings 16
Nutrition facts (Per serving) Calories 158 Fat 15g Protein 2.4g Carbs 4g
Ingredients:
- 6 oz. of dark chocolate chips sugar-free
- 1 Avocado medium
- 1/2 cup of butter
- 3/4 cup of blanched almond flour
- 1/2 cup of stevia
- 1 teaspoon of vanilla essence
- 1/4 cup of unsweetened cocoa powder
- 2 whisked large Egg

Instructions:
- Preheat your air fryer at 350°F. Line and lightly butter a glass baking dish with foil or parchment paper.
- Melt the butter and chocolate in a double boiler over low flame. (Bring a saucepan of water to the boil, then place the butter and chocolate in a heatproof bowl on top of the pot.) Cook, occasionally stirring, till the chocolate is melted.) Allow for a few minutes of cooling. (Alternatively, you can do this in the microwave.) Make sure not to burn it.)
- Combine the avocado, eggs, and vanilla extract in a high-powered blender or food processor. Puree till completely smooth. Once more, puree the melted butter/chocolate combination.
- Inside a small-sized mixing dish, combine the cocoa powder, almond flour, and sweetener. In the blender or food processor, stir in the dry ingredients with a spatula. Once blended, pulse a few times more, scraping down from the sides as needed. (Take care not to overmix.)
- Spread the batter evenly in the prepared baking pan. Smooth the finish with a spatula.
- Cook for about 15 minutes in the air fryer or until the brownies are set. The top should no longer be damp, but it should

still be very soft. Allow to cool completely before slicing.

5. Air-Fried Chocolate Hazelnut Lava Cake

Preparation time: 10 minutes
Cooking time: 12 minutes
Servings 2
Nutrition facts (Per serving) Calories 319 Fat 28.4g Protein 8.7g Carbs 10.8g
Ingredients:
- 2 tablespoons of dark chocolate chops sugar-free
- 1 tablespoon of butter
- 3 tablespoons of almond flour blanched
- 1 pinch of sea salt
- 2 tablespoons of hazelnut spread sugar-free
- 1 egg large
- 3 tablespoons of stevia
- 1/2 teaspoon of baking powder
- 2 1/2 tablespoons of cocoa powder (unsweetened)
- 1 tablespoon of Water
- 1/2 teaspoon of hazelnut extract

Instructions:
- Preheat your air fryer at 350°F.
- In a small pinch dish or ramekin, combine the chocolate chips and chocolate hazelnut spread. Freeze for 10-20 minutes or till the mixture is solid but not brittle. (You should also prepare it ahead of time and place it in the refrigerator for at least an hour.)
- Inside a small-sized bowl, microwave the butter for 30-40 seconds or till melted.
- Combine the egg, cocoa powder, and hazelnut essence in a mixing bowl. Stir vigorously till no lumps remain.
- Combine the almond flour, stevia, baking powder, and salt. Stir till smooth, scraping down the sides of the dish as needed. Half-fill ramekins with batter.
- Cook for around 10 to 12 minutes in the air fryer or till just set but still a touch sticky on top and the center is still gooey. You won't obtain the gooey molten lava center if they don't heat evenly or if you overheat them. Begin with less time and check in on a regular basis.

6. Air-Fried Low-Carb Banana Muffins

Preparation time: 10 minutes
Cooking time: 15 minutes
Servings 10
Nutrition facts (Per serving) Calories 295 Fat 27.4g Protein 9.3g Carbs 7.7g
Ingredients:
- 2 1/2 cups of almond flour blanched
- 1 teaspoon of banana extract
- 1/3 cup of unsweetened almond milk
- 1/2 cup of stevia allulose
- 3 eggs large (at room temperature)
- 3/4 cup of chopped walnuts
- 1/4 teaspoon of sea salt
- 1 1/2 teaspoons of baking powder
- 1/3 cup of melted butter

Instructions:
- Preheat your air fryer at 350°F. Line a muffin tin using parchment paper cupcake liners. (Use 12 for fewer calories and carbohydrates or 10 for larger muffin tops.)
- Inside a large-sized mixing bowl, combine the almond flour, allulose, sea salt, and baking powder.
- Combine the almond milk, melted butter, banana essence, and eggs inside a large-sized mixing dish. To the mixture, add 1/2 cup of chopped walnuts.
- Divide the batter evenly among the ramekins or muffin cups. Sprinkle with the remaining walnuts. If necessary, cook in batches in the air fryer basket.
- Cook for about 15 minutes in the air fryer or till the top is brown.

7. Air-Fried Lemon Raspberry Loaf

Preparation time: 10 minutes

Cooking time: 20 minutes
Servings 12
Nutrition facts (Per serving) Calories 166 Fat 14.7g Protein 5.7g Carbs 2.8g
Ingredients:
- 4 tablespoons of butter melted
- 200 grams of almond flour
- 1/4 cup of sugar substitute
- 1 teaspoon of lemon essence/extract
- 4 tablespoons of sour cream
- 100 grams of raspberries halved
- 1 teaspoon of vanilla essence
- 2 eggs whole
- 1/5 teaspoon baking powder

Instructions:
- Preheat your air fryer at 350°F. Line a loaf pan using parchment paper and spray with baking spray.
- Add together all of the ingredients stated above, except the raspberries, to a large-sized mixing dish and beat using an electric mixer till well combined.
- Add the raspberries and fold them in using a spatula.
- Spread the batter in the prepared loaf pan, then place it in the air fryer basket.
- Cook for around 15 to 20 minutes in the air fryer or until totally done.

8. Air-Fried Gluten-Free Cherry Cobbler with Hazelnut Topping

Preparation time: 10 minutes
Cooking time: 15 minutes
Servings 16
Nutrition facts (Per serving) Calories 106 Fat 7g Protein 3g Carbs 9g
Ingredients:
- 2/3 cup of erythritol, divided
- 1 teaspoon of baking powder
- 3/4 cup of hazelnut flour or ground hazelnuts
- 2 tablespoons of melted butter
- 6 cups of pitted Sour cherries
- 2 tablespoons of egg white
- 3/4 cup of blanched almond flour

Instructions:
- Preheat your air fryer at 350°F.
- Inside a mixing bowl, combine half of the erythritol and the sour cherries. Place the mixture in a foil-lined baking tray (or non-stick).
- Combine the almond flour, erythritol, hazelnut flour, and baking powder.
- Add the egg whites and mix till crumbly. Mix in the melted butter thoroughly. Crumble the flour mixture evenly over the berries. Transfer to the air fryer basket.
- In the air fryer, cook for about 15 minutes or till light golden brown.

9. Air-Fried Low-Carb Chocolate Chip Zucchini Muffins

Preparation time: 10 minutes
Cooking time: 20 minutes
Servings 12
Nutrition facts (Per serving) Calories 181 Fat 15g Protein 5g Carbs 8g
Ingredients:
- 3/4 cup of coconut flour
- 2/3 cup of ghee
- 8 oz. of shredded zucchini
- 1/2 cup of erythritol
- 6 eggs large
- 1/4 teaspoon of sea salt
- 1/2 cup of dark chocolate chips sugar-free
- 2 teaspoons of baking powder
- 1/2 teaspoon of vanilla extract

Instructions:
- Preheat your air fryer at 350°F.
- Inside a large-sized mixing dish, combine the sweetener, coconut flour, baking powder, & sea salt. Inside a mixing dish, combine the eggs, shredded zucchini, and vanilla essence. Toss everything together till fully incorporated. Add the melted coconut oil and stir till almost smooth.
- Fold the chocolate chips into the mixture. Allow 5 minutes for the batter to thicken.
- Fill the parchment liners all the way to the top with the batter. If desired, more chocolate chips can be sprinkled on top.

- Cook for around 15 to 20 minutes in the air fryer.

10. Air-Fried Blueberry Scones

Preparation time: 10 minutes
Cooking time: 20 minutes
Servings 8
Nutrition facts (Per serving) Calories 159 Fat 13g Protein 5g Carbs 8g
Ingredients:
For the scones:
- 1/4 cup of almond milk unsweetened
- 3 tablespoons of erythritol
- 1 cup of blanched almond flour
- 1/2 cup of blueberries
- 1/4 teaspoon of sea salt
- 2 tablespoons of melted coconut oil
- 1/4 cup of coconut flour
- 1 teaspoon of vanilla extract
- 1/2 teaspoon of baking powder
- 1 egg large

For the glaze:
- 2 tablespoons of blueberries
- 1 teaspoon of erythritol
- 1 tablespoon of melted coconut oil

Instructions:
- Preheat your air fryer at 350°F. Line an air fryer basket using parchment paper.
- Inside a medium-sized mixing bowl, combine almond flour, sea salt, coconut flour, erythritol, and baking powder.
- Inside a small-sized mixing bowl, combine the coconut oil, almond milk, vanilla essence, and egg. Fold together the wet and dry ingredients till a dough forms. (If the dough is too dry, gradually add a teaspoon of almond milk until it is flexible but not crumbly or stiff.) Fold in the blueberries after tossing them into the dough.
- Form a 1in (2.5 cm) thick disc of dough in the prepared air fryer basket. Each wedge should be cut into eight parts (like a pie or pizza). Separate the bits by approximately 1 inch (2.5 cm).
- Cook for 15 to 18 minutes in the air fryer or till golden brown.
- In the meantime, make the glaze. Puree the glaze ingredients in a blender. Strain through a fine-mesh strainer to catch (and discard) the blueberry skins. Drizzle the glaze evenly over the scones when they've completed baking. Allow to cool completely (scones and glaze will firm up as they cool).

11. Air-Fried Gluten-Free Coconut Macaroons

Preparation time: 5 minutes
Cooking time: 20 minutes
Servings 12
Nutrition facts (Per serving) Calories 135 Fat 11g Protein 1g Carbs 5g
Ingredients:
- 1 teaspoon of vanilla extract
- 1/3 cup of stevia
- 2 egg whites
- 1/4 teaspoon of sea salt
- 2 oz. of dark chocolate chips sugar-free
- 1/2 tablespoon of coconut oil
- 2 cups of shredded coconut unsweetened

Instructions:
- Preheat your air fryer at 350°F. Line an air fryer basket using parchment paper.
- Using a hand mixer set with a whisk attachment, whip the egg whites till medium-stiff peaks form. They can hardly move and not flow out if you tilt the mug.
- Add the sweetener, 1 to 2 teaspoons at a time, while constantly beating. Combine the vanilla extract and sea salt in a mixing bowl.
- Gently fold in the coconut flakes, taking care not to collapse the egg whites.
- Using a medium cookie scoop, place the batter in the lined air fryer basket.
- Cook for around 8 to 10 minutes in the air fryer.
- Follow these procedures to make the optional chocolate drizzle: Melt the chocolate chips and coconut oil together in the microwave or over a double boiler on the stove, stirring constantly, till smooth. To

finish, drizzle the chocolate over the macarons. Refrigerate to let the chocolate glaze to solidify.

12. Air-Fried Simple Low-Carb Pound Cake

Preparation time: 5 minutes
Cooking time: 20 minutes
Servings 12
Nutrition facts (Per serving) Calories 295 Fat 28.6g Protein 7.3g Carbs 5.5g
Ingredients:
- 2 1/2 cups of almond flour blanched
- 1/2 teaspoon of xanthan gum
- 4 eggs large
- 1/2 tablespoon of baking powder
- 1/4 teaspoon of sea salt
- 1 cup of softened butter
- 2/3 cup of stevia
- 1/2 tablespoon of vanilla extract

Instructions:
- Preheat your air fryer at 350°F. Line a loaf pan using parchment paper, leaving enough hanging over the two long edges.
- Inside a large-sized, deep mixing bowl, cream the butter and stevia using a hand mixer on high speed till fluffy.
- Beat in the eggs one at a time for 30 seconds after each addition. Incorporate the vanilla extract.
- Reduce the mixer speed to a medium-low setting. In a mixing dish, combine the almond flour, sea salt, and baking powder. If adding xanthan gum, evenly sprinkle it over the batter (do not pour it in) and mix on low speed till barely combined.
- Scrape down the edges of the dish. The batter will be thick and creamy. Smooth the batter into the loaf pan, smoothing the corners slightly.
- Cook for around 20 minutes in the air fryer.

13. Air-Fried Vanilla Cupcakes (Sugar-Free)

Preparation time: 10 minutes
Cooking time: 20 minutes
Servings 12
Nutrition facts (Per serving) Calories 309 Fat 29g Protein 7g Carbs 7g
Ingredients:
- 2 teaspoons of baking powder
- 1/3 cup of melted butter
- 2 1/2 cups of almond flour blanched
- 1/4 cup of almond milk unsweetened
- 1/2 cup of stevia
- 4 eggs large
- 1/2 tablespoon of vanilla extract

Instructions:
- Preheat your air fryer at 350°F. Line a muffin tin using cupcake liners.
- Inside a large-sized mixing bowl, combine the almond flour, stevia, and baking powder.
- Combine the eggs, almond milk, melted butter, and vanilla extract. Thoroughly combine.
- Using a big cookie or ice cream scoop, fill the muffin cups 3/4 full (a large cookie or ice cream scoop works well for this). Decorate the tops with raspberries if desired. Work in batches as necessary.
- Cook for around 15 minutes in the air fryer.

14. Air-Fried Low-Carb Lemon Bars

Preparation time: 10 minutes
Cooking time: 20 minutes
Servings 16
Nutrition facts (Per serving) Calories 166 Fat 14g Protein 6g Carbs 5g
Ingredients:
For the shortbread crust:
- 1/2 teaspoon of vanilla extract
- 1/4 cup of melted coconut oil
- 2 1/2 cups of almond flour blanched
- 1/4 teaspoon of sea salt
- 1 whisked egg large
- 1/4 cup of stevia

For the lemon filling:
- 4 eggs large
- 1 tablespoon of Lemon zest
- 1/3 cup of stevia powdered monk fruit allulose blend
- 3/4 cup of lemon juice
- 1/4 cup of blanched almond flour

Instructions:
- Preheat your air fryer at 350°F.
- Use parchment paper to line the pan, letting the paper hang over the edges.
- It is recommended to get the filling ready ahead of time so that it is ready to go as soon as the crust comes out of the air fryer. In a medium-sized bowl, whisk together the powdered sugar and the almond flour.
- The eggs, lemon juice, and lemon zest should all be mixed together till smooth. Take a break and put them down.
- The crust can be made by combining almond flour, salt, and sugar inside a large-sized dish.
- Then, include the egg, vanilla, and heated coconut oil. Although the dough appears brittle, it will remain together when pushed.
- Roll out the dough and pat it into a baking dish.
- Ten minutes is about right for cooking in an air fryer.
- When the crust is done in the air fryer, remove it and top it with the filling right away.
- Return to the air fryer and cook for an additional 10 minutes or till the filling has set but is still slightly pliable.
- Put it on the counter to cool down completely before you pick it up. Cover and chill for at least 2 hours before slicing.

15. Air-Fried Crunchy Butter Cashew Cookies

Preparation time: 5 minutes
Cooking time: 10 minutes
Servings 20 cookies
Nutrition facts (Per serving) Calories 90 Fat 7g Protein 2g Carbs 8g

Ingredients:
- 1/4 cup of sugar-free maple syrup
- 1 cup of creamy cashew butter
- 1/4 teaspoon of salt
- 1/4 cup of ground flaxseed

Instructions:
- Preheat your air fryer at 350°F.
- Inside a large-sized mixing dish, combine all of the ingredients. Form balls from level tablespoons. Flatten using a fork on an air fryer basket.
- Cook for around 9 to 10 minutes in the air fryer. Let cool on a wire rack.

16. Air-Fried Chocolate Almond Flour Cupcakes

Preparation time: 10 minutes
Cooking time: 15 minutes
Servings 10
Nutrition facts (Per serving) Calories 479 Fat 48g Protein 10g Carbs 11g

Ingredients:
- 1 1/4 cups of sugar-free chocolate frosting
- 3 eggs large
- 1/2 cup of stevia
- 6 tablespoons of cocoa powder
- 1/3 cup of softened butter
- 1 teaspoon of vanilla extract
- 1/2 cup of almond milk unsweetened
- 2 cups of almond flour blanched
- 1/2 tablespoon of baking powder
- 1/4 teaspoon of sea salt

Instructions:
- Preheat your air fryer at 350°F. Line 10 muffin cups using paper liners in a muffin pan.
- Inside a large-sized mixing dish, cream butter and sweetener using a hand mixer till fluffy.
- Inside a mixing bowl, combine almond flour, cocoa powder, sea salt, and baking powder. Combine the almond milk, eggs, and vanilla essence. Fill the cups with the mixture and place them in the air fryer. Cook in batches as necessary.

- Cook for around 15 minutes in the air fryer.

17. Air-Fried Crunchy Oatmeal Cookies

Preparation time: 10 minutes
Cooking time: 15 minutes
Servings 24
Nutrition facts (Per serving) Calories 122 Fat 11.5g Protein 3.6g Carbs 5g
Ingredients:
- 1/2 cup of Oat fiber
- 1 teaspoon of baking powder
- 3/4 cup of softened butter
- 2 eggs large at room temperature
- 1/2 teaspoon of xanthan gum
- 1 1/2 cups of almond flour blanched
- 1/2 teaspoon of sea salt
- 1 teaspoon of vanilla extract
- 3/4 cup of stevia brown monk fruit allulose
- 1 teaspoon of cinnamon
- 1/2 cup of hemp hearts

Instructions:
- Preheat your air fryer at 350°F. Line an air fryer basket using parchment paper.
- Inside a large-sized mixing dish, cream the butter and brown sugar together with a hand mixer till moist.
- Inside a separate medium-sized mixing bowl, combine the eggs and vanilla essence.
- Inside a large-sized mixing bowl, combine the almond flour, baking powder, oat fiber, cinnamon, sea salt, and xanthan gum (if using). (If using xanthan gum, spread it out evenly rather than pouring it in clumps.) Mix in the hemp seeds thoroughly.
- Using a medium cookie scoop, scoop the cookie dough onto the prepared air fryer basket, spreading it about two inches apart.
- Flatten the surface with a fork in various directions to a thickness of 1/4 to 1/3 inch (.6-.8 cm).
- Cook for 10 to 12 minutes in the air fryer or till the edges are brown and the cookies are just set.

18. Air-Fried Fluffy Cream Cheese Cookies

Preparation time: 10 minutes
Cooking time: 10 minutes
Servings 24
Nutrition facts (Per serving) Calories 110 Fat 10g Protein 3.4g Carbs 3.2g
Ingredients:
- 3 cups of almond flour blanched
- 1 tablespoon of sour cream (optional)
- 2 oz. of softened cream cheese
- 1/4 teaspoon of sea salt
- 2 teaspoons of vanilla extract
- 1/4 cup of softened butter
- 1 egg large
- 1/3 cup of stevia

Instructions:
- Preheat your air fryer at 350°F. Line an air fryer basket using parchment paper.
- In a hand or stand mixer, combine the cream cheese, butter, and sweetener and beat till frothy and light in color.
- Combine the salt, vanilla essence, and egg. If using, incorporate the sour cream (optional). Beat in the almond flour 1/2 cup (64 g) at a time. (The dough may be thick and crumbly, but it should hold together when squeezed together.)
- Using a medium cookie scoop (approximately 1 1/2 tablespoons, 22 mL volume), scoop dough balls onto the lined air fryer basket. Using your hand, create a flat surface.
- Cook for 10 to 12 minutes in the air fryer or till the edges are light golden brown.

19. Air-Fried Low-Carb Blackberry Cobbler

Preparation time: 10 minutes
Cooking time: 20 minutes
Servings 9

Nutrition facts (Per serving) Calories 154 Fat 12g Protein 5g Carbs 7g

Ingredients:

For the blackberry cobbler filling:
- 2 tablespoons of vital proteins grass-fed gelatin
- 1 lb. of Blackberries
- 1/3 cup of stevia
- 2 tablespoons of lemon juice

For the cobbler topping:
- 1/4 teaspoon of sea salt
- 1/2 teaspoon of vanilla extract
- 1/4 cup of stevia
- 1 cup of blanched almond flour
- 1/4 cup of coconut oil
- 1/2 teaspoon of baking powder

Instructions:
- Preheat your air fryer at 350°F.
- Combine the sugar, berries, and lemon juice inside a large-sized bowl. The gelatin can be added a little at a time; just sprinkle a spoonful on top, whisk it in, and then proceed with the rest.
- You can air fry berries if you fill a glass or nonstick baking dish midway with them.
- Coconut oil can be melted in a microwave or on the stovetop. Take the pan off the flame.
- Melt the coconut oil and add the vanilla extract to a small-sized bowl. Put the almond flour, baking soda, sugar, and salt in a bowl and mix well. The dough must have a crumbly texture, plenty of moisture, and a buttery flavor.
- To serve, crumble the dough all over the berries and leave some exposed. Insert the food into the air fryer.
- Add 15–20 minutes to the cooking time to ensure a golden top on the cobbler. If you prefer a thicker cobbler, let it sit for at least 10 minutes before serving, or let it cool to room temperature.

20. Air-Fried Sugar-Free Graham Crackers

Preparation time: 10 minutes
Cooking time: 10 minutes
Servings 12
Nutrition facts (Per serving) Calories 166 Fat 14.9g Protein 5.5g Carbs 4.6g

Ingredients:
- 5 tablespoons of melted butter
- 1/2 cup of stevia brown monk fruit allulose blend
- 2 cups of almond flour blanched
- 1.5 oz. of pork rinds
- 1/8 teaspoon of sea salt
- 2 teaspoons of cinnamon
- 1/2 tablespoon of vanilla extract
- 1 teaspoon of honey extract

Instructions:
- Preheat your air fryer at 350°F. Line an air fryer basket using parchment paper.
- Combine the pork rinds, almond flour, sweetener, cinnamon, and sea salt in a food processor. Pulse till everything is well blended, scraping down the edges as needed.
- Combine the vanilla, butter, and honey extract in a food processor and mix till a thick, sticky dough forms. Stopping to scrape down the sides as needed.
- Remove the dough from the food processor and roll it into a ball after it has reached a consistent consistency. Freeze for 10 minutes, or till the mixture is no longer sticky, then place in the refrigerator till ready to use.
- Place the dough ball between two large pieces of parchment paper. Roll out to a rectangle about 1/16 to 1/8 inch (1.5 to 3 cm) wide with a rolling pin.
- Cut the cracker dough into squares. Carefully peel the squares from the parchment and arrange them on the lined air fryer. Make holes with a toothpick or a fork. If you have some uneven dough around the edges, simply roll it out again and repeat. (You may need to cook in two batches if necessary.)
- Cook for around 10 to 15 minutes in the air fryer or till golden brown. Allow to cool before serving.

60 Days Meal Plan

1st Year

Days	Breakfast	Lunch	Snacks	Dinner
1	Healthy and Crunchy Breakfast Granola	Air Fried Healthy Salmon with Fennel Salad	Air-Fried Sugar-free Peanut Butter Cookies	Air Fried Root Vegetables
2	Classic Air Fried Breakfast Frittata	Air Fried Chicken Stuffed with Mozzarella and Asparagus	Air Fried Mozzarella Cheese Balls	Air Fried Stir-Fry Broccoli and Beef
3	Chanterelle Mushrooms and Zucchini Omelet	Air Fried Seafood Gratin	Air-Fried Gluten-Free Coconut Macaroons	Air Fried Chicken, Pepper, Bean, Tomato Roast
4	Scrambled Breakfast Eggs	Air Fryer Roasted Beef with Onion Gravy	Air Fried Seasoned Apple Chips	Air Fried Cheesy Herbed Cauliflower Quinoa Casserole
5	Breakfast Mashed Potato Pancakes	Air Fried Greek-Style Chicken Stir Fry	Cheesy Pizza Pepperoni Puffs	Air Fried Classic Meatloaf
6	Avocado Cauliflower Toast	Air Fried Pecan-Crusted Tilapia	Blueberry Scones	Air Fried Horseradish-Crusted Turkey Tenderloin
7	Sugar-Free Air fried Mix Berries Oatmeal	Air Fried Ratatouille	Air Fried Cheesy Cauliflower Bread Sticks	Air Fried Tikka-Style Fish
8	Tasty Breakfast Eggplant Pizza	Air Fried Eggplant Tomato Casserole	Air-Fried Magic Cookie Bars	Air-Fried Delicious Pork Medallions with Strawberry-Garlic Sauce
9	Cheesy Chicken, Carrot and Spinach Omelet	Air Fried Ranch Chicken Bacon Casserole	Air Fried Kale Chips	Air Fried Creamy Broccoli and Chicken Casserole
10	Cheesy Cauliflower Hash Browns	Air Fried Stuffed Flounder	Air Fried Cheddar-Sausage Bites	Air Fried Vegetable Tofu
11	Air Fryer Breakfast Apple Protein Muffins	Air Fried Zucchini and Halloumi Frittata	Air Fried Falafel	Air Fried Whole Roasted Chicken with Vegetables
12	Classic Air fried Egg Casserole	Air Fried Crispy Pork Chop Salad	Chewy Avocado Brownies	Air Fried Maple Mustard Beef Steaks
13	Scrambled Breakfast Eggs	Air Fried Delicious Chicken Gratin	Air Fried Garlic-Almond Crackers	Air Fried Roasted Broccoli Salad
14	Air Fried Sheet Pan Eggs	Air Fried Shrimp Scampi	Air Fried Sausage Stuffed Mushrooms	Air-Fried Sheet Pan Pork with Asparagus
15	Cheese and Ham Omelet	Air Fried Turkey Loaf	Air-Fried Low-Carb Chocolate Chip Zucchini Muffins	Air Fried Lemon-Oregano Chicken

16	Air Fried Breakfast Farmer's Casserole	Air Fried Salmon, Zucchini, and Carrot Patties	Air Fried Parmesan Cheddar Crisps	Air Fryer Roasted Veggie Bowl
17	Classic Air Fried Breakfast Frittata	Air Fried Foil Packed Lobster Tails	Air-Fried Low-Carb Banana Muffins	Air Fried Ranch Chicken Bacon Casserole
18	Air Fryer Cheese Picante Omelet Pie	Air Fried Classic Meatloaf	Air Fried Asparagus Tots	Air Fryer Tasty Zucchini Casserole
19	Tasty Breakfast Eggplant Pizza	Air Fried Whole Roasted Chicken with Vegetables	Air-Fried Low-Carb Lemon Bars	Air Fried Mussels with Herb and Lemon
20	Chanterelle Mushrooms and Zucchini Omelet	Air Fried Chicken, Pepper, Bean, Tomato Roast	Air Fried Pizza Muffins	Air Fried Creamy Tuna Casserole

2nd Year

Days	Breakfast	Lunch	Snacks	Dinner
1	Air Fried Buffalo Breakfast Egg Cups	Air Fried Chicken Stuffed with Mozzarella and Asparagus	Air-Fried Low-Carb Banana Muffins	Air Fried Maple Mustard Beef Steaks
2	Breakfast Portobello Pizzas	Air Fried Turkey Loaf	Air Fried Parmesan Cheddar Crisps	Air Fried Stir-Fry Broccoli and Beef
3	Air Fried Cheesy Egg Bites	Air Fried Beef Patties Smothered in Mushrooms	Air Fried Mozzarella Cheese Balls	Air Fried Chicken Meatballs
4	Cheese and Ham Omelet	Air Fryer Roasted Veggie Bowl	Air Fried Kale Chips	Air Fried Grilled Spiced Steak and Vegetables
5	Tasty Breakfast Eggplant Pizza	Air Fried Chicken, Pepper, Bean, Tomato Roast	Air Fried Pizza Muffins	Air Fried Asparagus with Cheese Sauce
6	Creamy Veggie Breakfast Frittata	Air Fried Steak with Chimichurri	Air Fried Seasoned Apple Chips	Air Fried Teriyaki Chicken
7	Air Fryer Cheese Picante Omelet Pie	Air Fried Beef Bulgur Patties	Air-Fried Low-Carb Lemon Bars	Air Fried Pecan-Crusted Tilapia
8	Scrambled Breakfast Eggs	Air Fried Steelhead Trout with Garlic, Lemon and Rosemary	Air-Fried Zucchini Bites	Air Fried Lemon-Oregano Chicken
9	Crustless Breakfast Caprese Quiche	Air Fried Whole Roasted Chicken with Vegetables	Air-Fried Chocolate Almond Flour Cupcakes	Air Fried Turkey Saltimbocca
10	Breakfast Mashed Potato Pancakes	Air Fried Scallion Sea Bass	Air Fried Cheddar-Sausage Bites	Air Fried Greek-Style Chicken Stir Fry
11	Air Fryer Breakfast Apple Protein Muffins	Air Fried Healthy Salmon with Fennel Salad	Air-Fried Sugar-free Peanut Butter Cookies	Air Fried Foil Packed Lobster Tails
12	Classic Air fried Egg Casserole	Air Fryer Roasted Cauliflower with Cilantro and Lime	Air Fried Cheesy Olives	Air-Fried Sheet Pan Pork with Asparagus

13	Air Fried Breakfast Farmer's Casserole	Air Fried Vegetable Tofu	Chewy Avocado Brownies	Air Fried Salmon, Zucchini, and Carrot Patties
14	Avocado Cauliflower Toast	Air Fried Delicious Chicken Gratin	Air Fried Deviled Eggs	Air Fried Root Vegetables
15	Air Fryer Avocado Egg Boat	Air Fried Chicken Meatballs	Air-Fried Magic Cookie Bars	Air-Fried Delicious Pork Medallions with Strawberry-Garlic Sauce
16	Scrambled Breakfast Eggs	Air Fried Ratatouille	Air-Fried Gluten-Free Coconut Macaroons	Air Fried Shrimp Scampi
17	Air Fried Buffalo Breakfast Egg Cups	Air Fried Teriyaki Chicken	Air-Fried Low-Carb Blackberry Cobbler	Air Fried Spicy Beef Strips with Peas
18	Breakfast Feta and Spinach Casserole	Classic Air Fried Green Bean Casserole	Air-Fried Crunchy Oatmeal Cookies	Air Fried Turkey Loaf
19	Avocado Cauliflower Toast	Air Fried Creamy Tuna Casserole	Cheesy Pizza Pepperoni Puffs	Air Fried Fajita-Flavored Flank Steak Rolls
20	Italian-Style Air Fried Breakfast Eggs	Air Fried Beef Patties Smothered in Mushrooms	Air Fried Kale Chips	Air Fried Spicy Beef Strips with Peas

3rd Year

Days	Breakfast	Lunch	Snacks	Dinner
1	Fluffy Air Fried Courgette Omelet	Air Fried Tikka-Style Fish	Air-Fried Chocolate Almond Flour Cupcakes	Air Fried Chicken Stuffed with Mozzarella and Asparagus
2	Italian-Style Air Fried Breakfast Eggs	Air Fried Turkey Saltimbocca	Air Fried Cheesy Crackers	Air Fried Scallion Sea Bass
3	Scrambled Breakfast Eggs	Air Fried Stir-Fry Broccoli and Beef	Air Fryer Loaded Faux-Tato Skins	Air Fried Steelhead Trout with Garlic, Lemon and Rosemary
4	Cheese, Egg and Bacon Roll-Ups	Air-Fried Delicious Pork Medallions with Strawberry-Garlic Sauce	Air-Fried Low-Carb Blackberry Cobbler	Air Fried Turkey Loaf
5	Breakfast Feta and Spinach Casserole	Air Fried Beef Patties Smothered in Mushrooms	Air Fried Cheesy Cauliflower Bread Sticks	Air Fried Mussels with Herb and Lemon
6	Air Fryer Breakfast Apple Protein Muffins	Air Fried Horseradish-Crusted Turkey Tenderloin	Air Fried Asparagus Tots	Air Fried Grilled Spiced Steak and Vegetables
7	Avocado Cauliflower Toast	Air Fryer Roasted Veggie Bowl	Air Fried Parmesan Cheddar Crisps	Air Fried Greek-Style Chicken Stir Fry
8	Healthy and Crunchy Breakfast Granola	Air Fried Eggplant with Cherry Tomatoes and Herbs	Air Fried Kale Chips	Air Fried Pecan-Crusted Tilapia

9	Tasty Breakfast Eggplant Pizza	Air Fried Chicken, Pepper, Bean, Tomato Roast	Air-Fried Zucchini Bites	Air Fried Spicy Beef Strips with Peas
10	Cheese and Ham Omelet	Air-Fried Sheet Pan Pork with Asparagus	Chewy Avocado Brownies	Air Fried Salmon, Zucchini, and Carrot Patties
11	Breakfast Mashed Potato Pancakes	Air Fried Root Vegetables	Apple Fritters with Cinnamon Sprinkle Topping	Air Fried Turkey Saltimbocca
12	Cheesy Cauliflower Hash Browns	Air Fried Parchment Wrapped Orange Tilapia	Blueberry Scones	Air Fried Delicious Chicken Gratin
13	Scrambled Breakfast Eggs	Air Fryer Tasty Zucchini Casserole	Air-Fried Low-Carb Banana Muffins	Air Fryer Roasted Beef with Onion Gravy
14	Creamy Veggie Breakfast Frittata	Air Fried Chicken Meatballs	Air-Fried Gluten-Free Coconut Macaroons	Air Fried Healthy Salmon with Fennel Salad
15	Sugar-Free Air fried Mix Berries Oatmeal	Air Fried Chicken Stuffed with Mozzarella and Asparagus	Air Fried Mozzarella Cheese Balls	Air Fried Eggplant Tomato Casserole
16	Chanterelle Mushrooms and Zucchini Omelet	Air Fried Maple Mustard Beef Steaks	Air-Fried Magic Cookie Bars	Air Fried Fajita-Flavored Flank Steak Rolls
17	Air Fried Buffalo Breakfast Egg Cups	Air Fried Turkey Saltimbocca	Air Fried Garlic-Almond Crackers	Air Fried Whole Roasted Chicken with Vegetables
18	Air Fryer Avocado Egg Boat	Air Fried Creamy Broccoli and Chicken Casserole	Air-Fried Sugar-Free Graham Crackers	Air Fried Beef Bulgur Patties
19	Tasty Breakfast Eggplant Pizza	Air Fried Beef Patties Smothered in Mushrooms	Air-Fried Sugar-free Peanut Butter Cookies	Air Fried Horseradish-Crusted Turkey Tenderloin
20	Breakfast Portobello Pizzas	Air Fried Steelhead Trout with Garlic, Lemon and Rosemary	Air-Fried Low-Carb Chocolate Chip Zucchini Muffins	Air-Fried Delicious Pork Medallions with Strawberry-Garlic Sauce

4th Year

Days	Breakfast	Lunch	Snacks	Dinner
1	Avocado Cauliflower Toast	Air Fried Creamy Tuna Casserole	Air Fried Mozzarella Cheese Balls	Air Fried Peri-Peri Chicken
2	Crustless Breakfast Caprese Quiche	Air Fryer Roasted Loaded Broccoli	Air Fried Sausage Stuffed Mushrooms	Air Fried Chicken Stuffed with Mozzarella and Asparagus
3	Sugar-Free Air fried Mix Berries Oatmeal	Air Fried Parchment Wrapped Orange Tilapia	Blueberry Scones	Air-Fried Plum-Glazed Pork Kebabs
4	Classic Air Fried Breakfast Frittata	Air Fried Shrimp Scampi	Air Fried Cheesy Crackers	Air Fried Vegetable Tofu

5	Creamy Veggie Breakfast Frittata	Air Fried Grilled Spiced Steak and Vegetables	Air-Fried Chocolate Almond Flour Cupcakes	Air Fried Beef Bulgur Patties
6	Chanterelle Mushrooms and Zucchini Omelet	Air Fryer Roasted Veggie Bowl	Apple Fritters with Cinnamon Sprinkle Topping	Air Fried Crispy Pork Chop Salad
7	Classic Air fried Egg Casserole	Air Fried Asparagus with Cheese Sauce	Air Fried Deviled Eggs	Air Fried Maple Mustard Beef Steaks
8	Scrambled Breakfast Eggs	Air Fried Stuffed Flounder	Air-Fried Gluten-Free Coconut Macaroons	Air Fried Eggplant with Cherry Tomatoes and Herbs
9	Cheesy Cauliflower Hash Browns	Air Fried Delicious Chicken Gratin	Air Fried Cheddar-Sausage Bites	Air Fried Lemon-Oregano Chicken
10	Air Fried Buffalo Breakfast Egg Cups	Air Fried COD with Asparagus	Air Fryer Loaded Faux-Tato Skins	Air Fried Foil Packed Lobster Tails
11	Air Fryer Avocado Egg Boat	Air Fried Healthy Salmon with Fennel Salad	Air-Fried Sugar-free Peanut Butter Cookies	Air Fried Roasted Broccoli Salad
12	Air Fried Cheesy Egg Bites	Air Fried Foil Packed Lobster Tails	Air-Fried Fluffy Cream Cheese Cookies	Air Fried Turkey Loaf
13	Air Fried Caprese Stuffed Avocado	Air Fried Steelhead Trout with Garlic, Lemon and Rosemary	Chewy Avocado Brownies	Air Fried Garlic-Mustard Chicken
14	Tasty Breakfast Eggplant Pizza	Air Fried Mussels with Herb and Lemon	Air-Fried Sugar-Free Graham Crackers	Air Fried Chicken Meatballs
15	Cheesy Chicken, Carrot and Spinach Omelet	Air Fried Zucchini and Halloumi Frittata	Air-Fried Low-Carb Lemon Bars	Air Fried Buttery Maple Chicken
16	Low-Carb Air Fried Garlic Bread	Air Fried Whole Roasted Chicken with Vegetables	Air Fried Pizza Muffins	Air-Fried Sheet Pan Pork with Asparagus
17	Crustless Breakfast Quiche	Air Fried Turkey Loaf	Air Fried Cheesy Olives	Air-Fried One-Pan Pork and Squash
18	Breakfast Feta and Spinach Casserole	Air-Fried Delicious Pork Medallions with Strawberry-Garlic Sauce	Cheesy Pizza Pepperoni Puffs	Air Fried Ratatouille
19	Scrambled Breakfast Eggs	Air Fried Chicken Stuffed with Mozzarella and Asparagus	Air-Fried Low-Carb Chocolate Chip Zucchini Muffins	Air Fried Salmon, Zucchini, and Carrot Patties
20	Air Fried Buffalo Breakfast Egg Cups	Air-Fried Plum-Glazed Pork Kebabs	Air Fried Kale Chips	Air Fried Eggplant Tomato Casserole

CONCLUSION

An air fryer will become an absolute need if you follow a bariatric diet or have had bariatric surgery. The more you learn about how it can help you prepare your favorite dishes and the meals you've had to give up due to dietary or lifestyle changes, the more you'll want one in your own kitchen.

If you're on a bariatric diet, an air fryer can help you satisfy your food cravings without sacrificing too much of your healthy eating plan.

Using an air fryer can be a great way to prepare healthy meals without sacrificing flavor. You don't have to eat a lot of oil to enjoy deep-fried items if you love them. On top of all that, it's a safe and easy-to-use appliance. It's easy to feed your family healthfully by paying attention to what goes into their diet.

Bariatric eating habits and sticking to a rigorous diet plan require a lot of dedication when making lifestyle adjustments. An air fryer makes it possible to eat whatever you want without worrying about your health. With the help of an air fryer, the effort put into a bariatric diet will be worthwhile.

Made in the USA
Middletown, DE
23 October 2023

41276233R00073